QUILOMBOLA!

Series Editor
LÉONORA MIANO

Quilombola is a Brazilian word for the inhabitant of a maroon, or 'runaway-slave' community. The choice of this appellation is a tribute to those who, throughout human history, have stood up against oppression. However, there is more in this reference: it speaks both about freedom regained and about all the creative gestures that stemmed from that conquest. For those who had broken their chains, the *quilombo* was a place of reappropriation and reinvention of oneself.

It is by inviting writers and readers to practice *marronnage*— 'running away from slavery'—of thought, to shift their way of thinking, that the series **Quilombola!** stands out. This list of books is a space from which resonate insubordinate, inventive, provocative and unexpected voices. Whether artists, activists or intellectuals, the authors of **Quilombola!** bring a sensitive reflection on the world and forge new paths. Although focusing on sub-Saharan African and French-speaking Afropean expressions, we welcome minority points of view from other places too.

The series aims at making itself accessible to a large readership in order to promote a wider circulation of thought. It is on this condition that it will come to meaningful fruition.

Shades of Black

NATHALIE ETOKE

TRANSLATED BY GILA WALKER

LONDON NEW YORK CALCUTTA

Seagull Books, 2021

Originally written in French as *Nuances du noir* by Nathalie Etoke
© Nathalie Etoke, 2021

First published in English translation by Seagull Books, 2021

English translation © Gila Walker, 2021

ISBN 978 0 8574 2 853 0

British Library Cataloguing-in-Publication Data
A catalogue record for this book is available from the British Library

Typeset by Seagull Books, Calcutta, India
Printed and bound by Versa Press, East Peoria, Illinois, USA

CONTENTS

Living in Black and White

> Race has become metaphorical—a way of referring to and
> disguising forces, events, classes, and expressions of social
> decay and economic division far more threatening to the
> body politic than biological "race" ever was.
>
> Toni Morrison, *Playing in the Dark*[1]

Racial identity is a social, cultural, and political invention rooted
in relationships of domination. The white-supremacist projects at
the origin of contemporary geopolitical imbalances have upended
the lives of human groups on several continents. Some were com-
pletely wiped out, others were kept alive for purposes of capitalist
exploitation. The enslavement of people of sub-Saharan origin went
hand in hand with a will to dehumanize them that has persisted
across time and space. The transatlantic slave trade and colonization
were not historical parentheses. They were foundational events that
engendered the world in which I live. From a scientific standpoint,

---

1 Toni Morrison, *Playing in the Dark*: *Whiteness and the Literary Imagination* (New
York: Vintage Books, 1993), p. 63.

race's fictive origin is now a proven fact. Yet, the concept continues to have very real consequences on human destiny. Some people assert that Black people cannot be racist. Others bring up anti-white racism and hatred of the other. This way of speaking about racism comes down to hurling anathemas back and forth. The clash between Blacks and whites remains mistakenly dependent on an approach informed by resentment and morality that mask the real political problem—namely, the way society organizes itself. Living in black and white means recognizing the relationship of power-lessness and power, disadvantage and privilege that influence the way individuals live.

Dylann Roof's flight, after killing nine Black people in a church in Charleston, South Carolina, was short-lived. According to the police officers who caught him, the young white supremacist did not resist arrest. Roof was calm and silent; he simply complained that he was hungry. The men in uniform hastened to feed him. They drove him to a Burger King. No doubt, the criminal did not deserve to be subjected to a punitive diet. Tamir Rice, a Black twelve-year-old who was playing with a toy gun in a City of Cleveland public park, was not entitled to such lenient treatment. A police officer simply shot the boy down.

Roof and Rice are both Americans. One was treated with com-passion, the other with cruelty. When a white man commits a mass killing, the media talk of mental illness. They try to understand what drove him to put innocent people to death. The individual is not reduced to the sum of his deeds. He possesses a measure of humanity that is ours too. This mutual recognition should be uni-versal but it remains selective. When you describe the condition of Black people, many would rather shift the conversation to social class and common humanity. But if poverty sufficed to build bridges between human beings, the face of the world would have changed long ago. Donald Trump, Matteo Salvini, and Marine Le Pen are merely personifications of the racial exasperation that characterizes economically disadvantaged white populations that see themselves as left behind and disdained by a globalized bourgeois elite. A non-negligible portion of the extremist electorate thinks of itself firstly as white and only thereafter as poor. Racial identification transcends social status. It confers a power that, when expressed in the ballot box, testifies to a specific concern: that of maintaining hierarchy and privilege. Consequently, when I speak of the Black person in a white world, I am referring to the degradation at once human, social, and political of populations of African descent.

The end of slavery and decolonization did not put an end to racism or socioeconomic inequality. To say that Blacks are heirs to a historical sub-humanity does not mean that they define themselves in these terms. I am evoking here a way of emerging in a world where the person's humanity withstands the trial of dehumanization. It is the scandal of the human being treated as private property, a workhorse, a thing that can be sold, used, assaulted or killed just like that. In such a context, individuals live in an environment hostile to their development. The conquest of one's freedom is a fight against a vacuum and the loss of meaning. The dehumanized human being is condemned to resilience and combativeness. The celebration of the vital force that refuses to die must not obliterate the fact that it remains impeded. In the United States, for example, Black people have confronted the tribulations of life entrenched in barbed wire with nobility and temerity.

However, history abounds in unfortunate episodes where the success acquired through work, self-abnegation, discipline, and responsibility was simply annihilated.

Who can imagine the consternation mixed with anger and incomprehension that took hold of the residents of Black Wall Street in Tulsa, Oklahoma? These men and women saw their dream come true collapse before their very eyes. These descendants of slaves from the south had been forced by racial segregation laws to settle in Greenwood, northern Tulsa, yet they managed to piece together the small things that gave rise to a prosperous community. They had a bank, two movie theatres, three hotels, twenty-one restaurants, clothing and jewelry shops, a library, a taxi-and-bus company, public schools, six private planes, and two newspapers. The sun rose over Black Wall Street on that June 1, 1921, heralding a day full of promise. Then the news spread that Dick Rowland, a young nineteen-year-old Black man, had been arrested in the white section of Tulsa. It was claimed that he had attacked Sarah Page. He was accused of attempting to rape her. White people gathered in front of the police station to lynch Rowland. Black people came to lend him unwavering support. The clash between the two groups led to a flare-up of violence that left ten whites and two Blacks dead. The reprisals were bloody. Their hearts filled with hatred and rage, whites stormed Black Wall Street for sixteen hours of destruction, looting and killing. Nearly 300 Black people lost their lives. The model of a collective success that could have served as a source of inspiration for other descendants of slaves was forever gone and no one was brought to justice, no less condemned. Sarah Page refused to file charges against Dick Rowland. As it turned out, the main witness had lied.

I can hear people objecting that times have changed. Yet the problem of the autonomy of Black individuals continues to be posed. To believe that imperialist democracies will grant a place worthy of the name to the populations they oppressed is to accept a political system that condemns the dominated to mendacity. Today, the white-supremacist society that destroyed Black Wall Street demands that Black people adopt the fighting spirit of their ancestors. We are told that the descendants of slaves must find solutions to their social and economic marginalization and seize on the opportunities that abound in the United States of America. Individuals are responsible no doubt for their destiny, whence the importance of demonstrating resilience to adversity. However, a time comes when promoting autonomy, combativity, and personal responsibility on the periphery of or within an oppressive society is downright crazy or suicidal. We have to have the courage to transform the society radically so that it becomes an environment where all can live.

In face of the Black crowds that never cease to challenge imperialist democracies, voices rise to express boundless exasperation. Times have changed, they say. There was a Black president in the United States. Black doctors, engineers, writers, and professors are now part of the social landscape. The people who applaud, celebrate, and marvel at the progress accomplished only confirm the unexpected and out-of-the-ordinary nature of the presence of this handful of individuals in certain spaces. Because they are not readily imagined holding positions of authority, Barack Obama, Colin Powell, and Condoleeza Rice become fetishes of diversity or fig leaves covering racism. As Black personifications of white supremacy, their main mission is to protect and maintain the interests of American imperialism. Before the so-called invasion of immigrants, the former imperialist powers observed and profited from the post-colonial chaos. Those who complain about being invaded never cared about the lives that were being crushed in some remote place to ensure their well-being and prosperity, or about how their ancestors swarmed into territories inhabited by others.

Ever since the misery of the world has washed up on the shores of Europe, we are called upon to examine our common destiny: to survive or perish together. No one is safe. When you have the audacity to evoke slavery or colonization to disclose the hidden side of the Black condition, many will insist that you stop dwelling on dark times. The irenic attitude toward slavery and colonial history that they advocate is belied by current challenges and conflicts. Some right-thinking souls do not deem that the projects of imperialist domination were merely negative. Others equivocate by arguing that colonization belongs to the past, that their ancestors were not involved in the tragedies that oppressed Blacks, and that the whole matter is of great complexity. In a word, the white man has laid down his burden. Descendants of slaveholders and colonizers are not guilty of the crimes their ancestors committed but they are responsible for choosing to enjoy a heritage procured in an iniquitous manner and to maintain oppressive disparities (often by violence). If Black people still endure the torments of racism, it is because they live with individuals who shirk responsibility for the past while perpetuating exclusionary and dehumanizing practices whose roots were planted in the holds of slave ships and in the fertile soil of plantations and the colonies.

Specific relationships of violence, oppression, dispossession, and inequality underpin the modern world. Current conflicts are merely continuations of a past that isn't past. The past deals a blow to the present; it surfaces in the way we relate to ourselves and to others. Both in the United States and in the European nations experiencing unsolicited immigration, we are witnessing an ideological polarization around the racial question. Citizens or immigrants (legal or illegal), non-white individuals were considered foreigners whose presence was justified solely by their capacity to work, to be exploited, to bow and scrape without ever forgetting to express infinite gratitude. Today they embody a demographic and cultural threat: the enemy from within.

The Great Replacement theory has superseded the ideology of the Clash of Civilizations. It is no longer a matter of opposing the West and the global South, but of measuring the scope of a population change that, we are told, will gradually lead to the disappearance of European civilization. Terrorism, socioeconomic problems, the massive displacement of populations originating in the Middle East, North Africa, and sub-Saharan Africa are analyzed solely from the perspective of a threat. Donald Trump wanted to build a wall on the border between the United States and Mexico. Theorists of re-migration dream of a world in which they could simply send undesirable populations back to the lands of their ancestors.

Re-migration is not going to happen. It is too late. For centuries, enslaving and colonial countries seized territories that were not theirs, taking possession of the land, the men, the women and the children. They enriched themselves with no thought to tomorrow. No doubt they imagined that slavery and colonization would last forever. The past is an indication of the future. Out of the womb of death—the Middle Passage, slavery, and colonization—Black populations were born. Imperialist democracies were intended for a specific human group. The Proclamation of the Rights of (white) Man was perfectly compatible with the oppression of non-whites. When Blacks revolted in Haiti, the champions of the French Revolution forced them to pay the price of their freedom. The Americans occupied the first Black republic for nineteen years.

Centuries of oppression and domination by white people have forged a colossal and narcissistic white ego that has clothed the Black person in a bereaved humanity. People of sub-Saharan descent who are born and raised in the West experience an exteriority that they have not sought. The history attached to the color of their skin predates their existence. If freedom is "the sum of acts and operations by which man emerges as human,"[2] and race is a straitjacket that reduces the human to nothing, Black individuals are confronted with a paradoxical choice: to exist as a Black or/and as a human being? In imperialist democracies, Black identity remains the depositary of a diminished humanity. James Baldwin was fully aware of this, when he wrote a letter to his nephew that reads like a handbook for Black resilience in a racist America. In it he lovingly instructs the young man without denying a frightening truth: "We cannot be free until they are free. God bless you, James, and Godspeed."[3] It is with these hardly reassuring words that Baldwin closes his epistle.

The freedom of Blacks is chained to that of whites. As demoralizing as this observation may seem, it is not so much a matter of pessimism or resignation, but simply a statement of the psychological dimension of political oppression. Whites have to liberate

---

2 Boulaga Fabien Eboussi and Kisukidi Nadia Yala, "Poursuivre le dialogue des lieux," *Rue Descartes* 81 (2014): 84–101; here, p. 94.

3 James Baldwin, *The Fire Next Time* (New York: Dial Press, 1963), p. 10.

their imagination from the inhuman creature they had to invent to justify their voracious appetite for conquest, domination, exploitation, and violence. No one can do this work for them. The inhuman creature is trapped in a physical and mental prison whose key he alone possesses. Consequently, Black individuals must refuse to see themselves in the warped mirror of a malaise that is not theirs.

In this regard, let us take a brief look at the controversy over blackface. As a tribute to the Harlem Globetrotters, the soccer player Antoine Griezmann dressed up as a Black basketball player. Every five years, a Night of the Blacks is held as part of the carnival in the city of Dunkirk: aside from covering their faces in black makeup, participants wear raffia skirts and feathered head-dresses, and sport the carefully drawn blood-red lips of a hideous but jovial cannibal. The carnival in the Belgian town of Ath, which has existed since the Middle Ages and figures on the UNESCO heritage list since 2008, was recently at the heart of a racial controversy. One of the principal attractions is "the savage"—a character created in 1856. Chained and agitated, it is supposed to evoke "the exoticism of the nineteenth century," but it is also intended "to make the public laugh and to scare the children."[4] Some years ago, police officers in the Kremlin Bicêtre outskirts of Paris held a costume party to celebrate Africa. Eager to share this moment of exceptional joy, they posted photos of the private event on Facebook. One of the participants can be seen seating cross-legged on banana leaves. In his lap are two bananas that he has not had the time to eat since he is too busy scratching his armpits. Megyn Kelly, an American

---

4 According to an article in the newspaper *Le Figaro*: "Un carnaval belge accusé de racisme, l'Unesco sommé de le retirer de sa liste," August 23, 2019. Available at: https://bit.ly/3izBa6V (last accessed on August 11, 2020).

journalist, lost her job after having maintained that there was nothing wrong with dressing up as a Black person for Halloween.

Painting your face and body black and acting out stereotypes is a racist act. The white actors who created blackface performed in minstrel shows. These shows spread the image of Blacks as stupid, comic, and ugly but endowed with a gift for dancing. The joy of Blacks was coupled with a propensity for merriment. Their condition as slaves must have been satisfactory,[5] after all—what else would account for their cheerful disposition? The joie de vivre, often magnified in minstrel shows, would give way from time to time to fleeting tragicomic moments of sorrow. Imperialist democracies have grown accustomed with annoyance to hearing impulsive voices crying racism on TV. At the risk of shocking antiracists, I must say that the blackfaces provoke neither anger nor indignation in me. I refuse to see myself in the mirror of a debased humanity that is not mine. The pathetic, grotesque spectacle of people enjoying the degradation of another human group reveals a devastating malaise of which they are still unaware. To this very day, the dominant do not acknowledge their intimate wound: the harm inflicted on the other is the reflection of the self. If the inhuman creature they invented vanished from their imagination, what would become of this white crowd painted black? For the space of a moment as long as eternity, it would be disoriented. By accepting to lose themselves, the straying multitude would rediscover the road to freedom that leads to the creation of a humanity that is one and indivisible. Nobody can do this work on their behalf.

---

5 After the American Civil War, descendants of slaves had access to theater companies. Their participation gave a stamp of authenticity to the racist entertainment.

Living in black and white also means recognizing the psychological and political imprint of a modern world founded on a system of domination whose binarity masks internal divisions. Racial homogeneity obliterates historical, social, cultural, and political differences between populations of African descent, from sub-Saharan Africa, from the Caribbean, from Latin America, from Europe and from the United States of America. Yet tensions divide these different groups. The common phenotype does not mean that these heterogeneous populations feel a sense of belonging to a people, and even less that they believe in the same historical destiny. They have divergent interests and degrees of success. Enmity now supplants the desire to forge a collectivity informed by shared hopes and common values. Only the upheavals caused by tragic news events spark occasional outbursts of solidarity.

The synonymy between Black race and victimization reduces the problem of freedom to a matter of human rights and access to citizenship. From a political standpoint, Blacks were stripped of their rights. The idea of the human being in the Western sense of the term goes hand in hand with the exploitation of Blacks and the deprivation of their civil rights. In the United States, for example, before the Constitution was amended in 1865, it stipulated that Blacks counted as three-fifths of a human being. The first *Code Noir* (Black Code), established by Jean-Baptiste Colbert and published in 1685, two years after his death, allowed French law to deny the humanity of sub-Saharans by codifying the modalities of their social domination on plantations in the French overseas colonies. The *Code de l'indigénat* continued this work of denegation and exclusion of oppressed populations. This legal framework established a hierarchy between white French citizens and Black

French subjects—the colonizer versus the colonized—thereby institutionalizing racial inequality, forced labor, violence, and injustice. People of sub-Saharan origin, first reduced to slavery and then colonized, lived outside the social and legal structures that recognize and guarantee the sacredness of human life.[6]

Since the abolition of slavery and decolonization, and against a backdrop of globalization, the political status of the Black individual is not self-evident: to assert that "Black Lives Matter" is to admit that they do not matter while maintaining that they should. I embrace the paradoxical contours of this observation. From this forced embrace emerges the difficult duty of creating a world where the power to act upon one's destiny can overturn the forces of destruction.

---

6 The Afro-pessimist writer Frank B. Wilderson argues that there is a consensus that Africa is populated by "sentient beings who are outside the global community." He goes so far as to say that they are "socially dead." He adds that Black Americans are confronted with a paradigm of oppression that offers no way out ("Blacks and the Master/Slave Relation" [2015] in *Afro-Pessimism: An Introduction*, Minneapolis, MN: Racked & Dispatched, 2017, pp. 20–22). Afro-pessimism elaborates a "grammar of suffering" that rejects all forms of transcendence. In a white-supremacist world, the existence of Blacks is trapped in oppressive structures. Violence and death are constitutive of a life whose main characteristic is that it is not fully lived. The capacity to act is plainly limited not to say non-existent. While whites are human, Blacks cannot divest themselves of their status as slaves or descendants of slaves.

CHAPTER 1

To Be Situated

> I inhabit a sacred wound
> I inhabit imaginary ancestors
> I inhabit an obscure will
> I inhabit a long silence
> I inhabit an irremediable thirst
> I inhabit a one-thousand-year journey
>
> Aimé Césaire, "Lagoonal Calendar"[1]

WHERE ARE YOU FROM?

This was a question I would have to answer often when I was living in France.[2] A few years ago, when I went back to Paris for spring holidays, I had an exchange with the immigration officer who was checking my travel documents. Knowing nothing whatever about

---

1 *Aimé Césaire: Lyric and Dramatic Poetry, 1946–82* (Clayton Eshleman and Annette Smith trans) (Charlottesville: University Press of Virginia, 1990), p. 83.

2 [The typical French way of putting this question to anyone with a non-French accent or any person of color is: "Vous êtes de quelle origine?" Literally: What is your origin?—Trans.]

my life, he nonetheless filtered it through a whole series of preconceived notions. Finding it difficult to reconcile my citizenship, my
command of French and the fact that I was living in the United
States, he felt obliged to interrogate me: "You're Cameroonian?
From what I hear, it sounds like you were educated here. You have
no accent. Do you really live in the United States? What do you
do there? You have a Green Card? How did you manage to get one?
You're a professor in a university?" On the other side of the Atlantic,
the racial prejudices of people I meet are challenged by my uncer-
tain accent. I am Black but the way I express myself reveals both a
troubling foreignness and a proximity. Americans have a hard time
situating me. They imagine that I am Haitian or from one of the
former British colonies in the Caribbean, or sometimes perhaps
Nigerian or Ghanaian. This desire to identify what is not familiar
derives no doubt from a human need.

After twenty-four years of living abroad, I observe that my
accent and the color of my skin trigger intrusive conversations in
which I participate in spite of myself. On the phone with the sales
department of my Internet service provider or in the classroom
with students, my accent makes me the object of an insatiable
curiosity that I cannot evade. I deviate from the norm and I frus-
trate expectations. The most insignificant encounter becomes the
pretext for just about anybody to question me about my life choices
and my journey as an immigrant. Everyone thinks I will be
delighted to answer them since they are taking an interest in me.
Does your accent or skin color entitle people to ask you where you
were born, how long you have been in America, why you are here,
if you like it, and if you go back often? If the person happens to
know another African, they will tell you: "I met a Senegalese," or

"I was in high school with a Cameroonian." If they have been to Kenya or South Africa, you will be treated to often bizarre anecdotes that you did not ask to be told. Yet you have to satisfy the egotism of a stranger by showing that you value their experience.

African Americans, as a minority in a white space, are also subjected to these conversation-cum-interviews. To justify their presence in professional circles where Blacks are few and far between, they are pressed to disclose the biographic details of their lives. When you are Black, sooner or later, you will have to tell the story of how you came to be where you are. There is no getting around it. The questioner decides whether you deserve to be there or not, accepts you with enthusiasm or tolerates the situation. The opinion of Black people is required on certain subjects. The words of one Black person stand for all Blacks. They never express the individuality of the speaker. The person's subjectivity is collective, associated with that of other anonymous people, a group that, even though it is part of society, continues to be apprehended from the perspective of an inextricable foreignness.

Being summoned to explain my presence on the basis of my appearance led me to think about issues of nationality, identity, belonging, and language. We do not choose our skin color nor do we choose the country or social class into which we are born. Nevertheless, these contingent characteristics have consequences on the individual's future. I was born in Paris to Cameroonian parents who saw no interest in transmitting the language of our ancestors. As a result, French is the first language I spoke at home. After nineteen years in the United States, I now use English in everyday life. I grew up in a post-colonial dictatorship that became a democratorship—a mix of democracy and dictatorship. My family genealogy is rooted in Douala, a port city located on the Atlantic coast at the mouth of the Wouri River.

In Cameroon, everyone is Black so no one is. A friend who had lived for more than a decade in England told me that his definitive move back to Nigeria had a more liberating effect on his son than he could have imagined. The eight-year-old had never been in his parents' country. At the Lagos airport, the boy silently observed the hustle and bustle around him. Surprised by the wide-eyed smile that my friend saw on his son's face, he asked him if everything was alright. "I adore this place," the son replied. "There are Blacks everywhere!" Because he had spent the first years of his life in a predominantly white country, this boy had developed a sense of self as being in the position of a minority. In England, his Nigerian and Yoruba identity was expressed in the private sphere. Otherwise, he was simply Black.

This was not the situation I faced. My childhood and teenage years were not marked by racial antagonism. As one of four girls in my family, the gender question was never an obstacle to my personal accomplishment. The public schools I went to made me sensitive to class differences and ethnic diversity. The surname evokes a people, a language, a history, and a referential framework. Ethnicity is politicized because it often plays a decisive role in the social, political, and economic construction of the post-colonial nation. In Cameroon, the regional balances are respected more or less in the distribution of power. However, the sharing of the national pie does not eradicate ethnic and linguistic antagonisms. The regime had the intelligence to choose its agents, who now constitute a ruling caste. As a result, a multi-ethnic oligarchy exists that participates in state banditry and in repressing freedom. In spite of identitarian issues rooted in relations of power and domination, my belonging to the Douala people did not give rise in any way to an ethnic consciousness that would condition my relationship with other Cameroonians.

BLACK IMMIGRANT WOMAN

I did my undergraduate and master's degree studies in France, and went on for my PhD in the United States where I have been living since 2001. Two years after Donald Trump's election, I applied for American citizenship. Why all these personal details? To indicate *where I speak from* and *what I'm speaking about*. Since I left Cameroon in 1995, my gender, my race, my citizenship, and my social status have constituted categories of identification and classification that have forced me to examine my situation. In the years before I had a Green Card, when I would come back to the States from a trip, I would have to check the "nonresident-alien" box. Non-resident foreign nationals are authorized to enter and stay in the United States on a temporary basis. They have documents that specify the reason for their presence and the length of their stay. The meanings of the term alien extend beyond the legal vocabulary in reference to immigration. It also refers to the unfamiliar, the other, a being from another world or planet. When you think about it, in a white world, the Black person is in many respects an extra-terrestrial being, an alien from a planet peopled by non-humans or sub-humans that it is the task of the West to elevate to the rank of human.

I became a *Black* when I arrived in France. The use of the English term instead of *noir* to refer to Black people of African or

Afro-Caribbean descent manifests a fascination for the thingifica-
tion and consumption of Black (American) bodies in entertainment and sports. It also testifies to a process of distancing that leads
to a denial of race as a discriminating social and political marker.
It is a mechanism of avoidance and self-protection that conceals
the French malaise with regard to the racial question. The Black
American exudes a singular aura that has been established in the
imaginary of *jouissance*. Their athletic and musical exploits are a
source of joy and pleasure. In choosing to live in France, Black
Americans break free from the American racial stranglehold. There
they become objects of appreciative curiosity. When I first came to
the United States, some Black Americans would ask me why I was
in Chicago. I had left the land that embraced Blacks at a time when
racist America was lynching them. France had welcomed Josephine
Baker, Nina Simone, James Baldwin, Richard Wright, and Sidney
Bechet. Paris had been the European jazz capital. After World War
II when interracial relations were criminalized in their native country, Black Americans married white women and chose to live in
France. The experience of a life unfettered by institutional racism
was possible. France offered hospitality to the Black intellectual
and artistic elite.

There has been a longstanding love affair between the French
and African Americans founded on the desire to escape the racial
difficulties of their respective nations. By Americanizing people of
sub-Saharan origin, the French create a pacified social situation in
which race is stripped of its conflictual charge. Memory blindness
is coupled with scotomization: the individual represses a painful
reality that her conscious mind cannot examine. Given the linguistic protectionism in Victor Hugo's homeland, I've always found

suspect the French use and normalization of the term *Black*. It has a positive aura that nothing dissipates. Our discursive practices evidence our relationship to the world, to the other, and to ourselves. I have never introduced or defined myself as a *Black*. When a white French person refers to me as such, they are forcing me to see myself through a term that I did not choose. I am "*une femme noire*," not a *Black*.

My interlocutors mean no harm. Most of the time, I do not correct them. In any case, these well-intentioned souls would not understand. In order to deny that they might sometimes, given their calamitous destiny, feel bitter, sad, or angry, Black people are expected to demonstrate an attitude in keeping with their warm, friendly image. Whereas the term *Black* is supposed to qualify people of African descent, it actually reflects first and foremost a discourse on oneself. The unequivocal message being sent by white French people who use it is that they are open-minded and antiracist. The forced racial designation betrays a losing power struggle. It is never a question of me, but always of the person designating me. Insofar as I do not have control over the discursive parameters of this identity as a *Black*, my body becomes the receptacle of preconceived notions, stereotypes, and expectations—be they negative or positive. The word is invested with a host of fantasies rooted in an imaginary that is not mine. In this view of things, I am the object of the white gaze. Imprisoned in a configuration of this type, a form of paranoia can develop, especially in relationships of seduction. Certain compliments or comments are offensive because they seem to come from a legacy of slavery and colonialism in which Black women exist only through an exotic hypersexuality. They are ascribed an animal femininity that enraptures or repels.

People in America often find the anger of Black women incomprehensible. Why, they wonder, are they always angry? Does their anger invalidate the veracity and depth of what they are saying? The focus on tone and emotion is part of a process of delegitimizing the discourse. Without ever tackling the problem raised, the conversation is shifted to a dishonest discussion about civility. In the American media, there is an observable tendency to devalue, discredit, or deny the life experience of Black individuals. In France, they often prefer to discuss the issues among whites, with the good side pitted against the bad. On the rare occasions when Blacks speak out publicly on questions that concern them primarily, they are accused of being extremists, *communautaristes*,[3] and even anti-white racists. The telling of the experience by the individual who is living through it is inadmissible because it provokes a narcissistic wound. It is an unbearable diatribe.

Black populations hold up an unflattering mirror to Western democracies, casting a shadow on the ideals upon which they are founded. Whether it is a matter of slavery, of colonization, or of the postcolony,[4] these foundational moments in the development

---

3 [The French term *communautarisme* has the pejorative sense of identifying with one's own particular community and setting it apart from or giving it precedence over the universal or the national.—Trans.]

4 In the context of this essay, the term "postcolony," written without a hyphen, is a construct theorized by Achille Mbembe in reference to the period following colonization. It appears for the first time in a collection of his essays titled *De la postcolonie. Essai sur l'imagination politique dans l'Afrique contemporaine* (Paris: Karthala, 2000), translated into English as *On the Postcolony* (Berkeley: University of California Press, 2001), in which Eurocentric universalism is critiqued. Mbembe examines sovereignty, power, and *commandement* on a land where the face of terror and oppression is no longer that of the colonizer. He explores the fractures and tensions within which Africa is being called upon to emerge in the future.

of people of African descent are at odds with the idea that all human beings are born free and equal in dignity and in rights. When people of sub-Saharan origin muse about their past and present, they may cultivate a sad, angry consciousness. Speaking out in public externalizes the feeling of revolt against the lies and absurdity of living oppressed in a society that swears by freedom alone, of being a sub-human in the land of human rights. Immured in incommunicability, these tragic contradictions punctuate the lives of the descendants of slaves and of colonized people, conscious as they are of belonging to a world that accepts them only insofar as it can exclude them.

I situate myself at the intersection of three countries: Cameroon, France, and the United States. They are the anchorage points of an antiphonic reflection on race. I lived the first seventeen years of my life in the bosom of a loving family in my ancestral country. I did not, however, grow up in a cavern, sheltered from the degrading images that certain French humorists adored. We had access via satellite dishes to a variety of TV channels. Seen from Cameroon, the stereotypical, racist representations seemed simply ludicrous, so grotesque I would laugh at them. Michel Leeb, Patrick Sébastien, and Elie Kakou[5] never sparked any anger or resentment from me. I sang "We are the World" and "Ethiopie"[6] without thinking that they concerned me. I was not dying of hunger. I had learned in primary school that Cameroon had food self-sufficiency. True or false? At the time, I did not ask myself this

5 [Three popular comedians on French TV.—Trans.]

6 [In 1985, in the wake of the release of "We Are the World," popular French singer-songwriters recorded "Ethiopie," also in response to the famine in Ethiopia.—Trans.]

type of question. Armed conflicts were localized, at once close and remote. The domestic workers in my parents' home were often from Chad. Having fled the civil war in their homeland, they had found refuge in Cameroon. François and Jacob—those were their names— spoke with a sadness tinged with humor about what they had gone through to escape death. When the Cameroonian army rounded up people in their neighborhood early one morning, the two men arrived at our place frightened but happy to have evaded expulsion. In 1994, the genocide of the Tutsis in Rwanda stunned me. We got the news from the French media. I did not know why but the way the events were told seemed suspicious to me. The shocking images left a lasting imprint in my mind. From the summit of my seventeen years, I wondered about the passiveness of the African governments. In Cameroon, as everywhere else, life went on.

The continued gap between my life and the TV images of an Africa beset by war and famine did not cause me any confusion. I always knew that truth was elsewhere. I owe my self-esteem, self-confidence, and love for the continent where I grew up to my family and to the Cameroonian teachers who guided me on the road to knowledge of myself and the world. Proving that the image others had of me was false was never my concern. People often expect Black intellectuals to present a positive representation of the experience of populations from which they originate. I refuse to sacrifice my critical spirit to this belief. To explore the dark side of sub-Saharan people is to recognize their humanity.

After twenty-five years living in the West, it is all too obvious to me that the Eurocentric representations of African violence and misery essentialize universal situations. African conflicts are seen as ethnic, not human. Poverty is not seen as a matter of poor governance or the influence of international monetary organizations, but as reflecting a deficit of humanity. The false description of the African experience extends into the malicious representation of what Africa has become in Europe and in the United States. The media speak of ethnic violence in the French *banlieues* or of Black-on-Black crime in the disadvantaged neighborhoods of the United States. Young white Americans randomly kill other whites. Sometimes, before such mass murders, they may butcher their own families. No one speaks of white-on-white crime. It is always a matter of a deranged gunman or a teenager traumatized by bullying in school.

The racial imbalance in the treatment of the human shapes Afro-diasporic identity. The age of innocence is ephemeral. Black Westerners are born and raised in a society that instills a sense of inferiority in them. Asserting or recognizing the value of one's existence becomes a titanic struggle. What shatters self-esteem makes whole. Sometimes, people sink into hatred of the self and of the other who rejects them. Trying hard to adopt the traits of the dominant culture, they can also become intoxicated by the wine of assimilation that never yields the anticipated effect: complexion is an indelible stain that makes it impossible to blend into the white mass.

When I speak of race, I am referring not to what is seen but to what the subject experiences in a white-supremacist world. The degradation, marginalization, and criminalization of Black people guarantees the stability and permanence of the structures of domination. To accuse Blacks of being obsessed with race is to refuse to admit that they are forced to develop a relationship to a life wherein racism brings added suffering to the human condition.

As a professor of francophone and Africana studies in an American university, my African origins and my academic interests put me in a situation that is at once unique and ambivalent. The academic system perceives me as a Black woman, thereby classifying me in a racial category according to criteria I did not choose. Since I am inevitably attached to a group of oppressed and ostracized populations, professional opportunities open up for me. With the rise of identity politics bound up with a need for recognition, reparation, and justice, some African Americans may regard my social position as a form of injustice and imposture: here I am, a Cameroonian immigrant, occupying a position that should have gone to a descendant of slaves.

In immigrating to the United States, I inherited a racial, cultural, political, and social history. However, my personal path also echoes the individualism of the American dream. According to this patriotic fiction, the United States is the land where anything is possible if you work hard enough, regardless of race, class, gender, or sexuality. Although I am not a descendant of slaves, we have a common phenotype. The color of my skin lodges me in age-old dynamics of power of inclusion and exclusion. The dividing lines between the dominant and the dominated are at once porous and impermeable. The visibility of successful Black people is a smoke screen. People will have us believe that the fact that a Black person can climb the social ladder means racism is not worthy of mention anymore; in this perspective, class transcends race. But the tendency to set the supposed prosperity of a few Black people up as models should alert us to the dangers of certain mechanisms of representation. Individual successes are forged to the detriment of the vast majority of Black people who live in poverty. Indeed, even if some of these individuals came from poor backgrounds, the success of a handful of exceptions contributes neither to the eradication of racism nor to the destruction of economic disparities.

Furthermore, all that glitters is not gold. To take a case in point, in academia, Black women are overrepresented in precarious temporary positions that offer no prospect of tenure. They make up 2 percent of university full professors in the United States.[7] In England, there are 25 Black women and 90 Black men out of a total of 19,000 professors.[8] And in France? Mum's the word, for ethnic statistics are forbidden. In the United States, the process of evaluation for advancement at a university is particularly challenging. Tenure is usually granted after six to seven years. Because some of our white colleagues think our presence in academia is due to affirmative action or to policies in favor of diversity, we are "presumed incompetent."[9]

There are indeed recruitment practices aimed at minorities. In the course of my career, I have been a member of several hiring committees. The message from the institution was unambiguous: diversity was the priority. Yet, the fact that we have been hired as Black women—a double minority—does not mean that we are not

---

7 Marlene L. Daut, "Becoming Full Professor While Black," Chronicle of Higher Education, July 28, 2019. Available at: https://bit.ly/2KWEP39 (last accessed on December 1, 2020).

8 Richard Adams, "UK Universities Making Slow Progress on Equality, Data Shows," *Guardian*, September 7, 2018. Available at: https://bit.ly/3oofRIv (last accessed on December 1, 2020).

9 Gabriella Gutiérrez Y Muhs, Yolanda Flores Niemann, Carmen G. González, and Angela P. Harris (eds), *Presumed Incompetent: The Intersections of Race and Class for Women in Academia* (Logan: Utah State University Press, 2012).

qualified to exercise our profession. In comparison with our white colleagues, the institution is always asking us for more.[10] Our fields of research, which do not always correspond to the criteria imposed by traditional disciplines whose colonial import is disregarded, are often undervalued or delegitimized. To prove that we deserve the position we occupy, we have to go beyond the requirements of our function.

Middle class and Black, integrated and excluded, I enjoy a privileged status in an oppressive system. This existential paradox highlights the way in which imperialist democracies create social, economic, political, and cultural mechanisms through which the hyper-visibility of Blacks masks their invisibility. During my first year of teaching in a small liberal arts college in Connecticut, I was invited to a memorable lunch. On campus for a semi-annual meeting, the members of the Board of Trustees wanted to meet the regiment of recently hired professors. Special attention was given to my colleagues and me. When they saw us walk into the banquet hall, the decision makers, all white men and women, over sixty for the most part, smiled with satisfaction. Each of the new professors was given a choice place. We were asked about our origins and our academic backgrounds.

Enchanted by the anecdotes we shared of our lives and very proud of their new acquisitions, the members of the Board of Trustees looked fixedly at us. All the colors of the American ethnic rainbow were represented. We were the roster of Benetton models, the most diverse in the history of the institution created in 1911.

---

10 Patricia A. Matthew (ed.), *Written/Unwritten: Diversity and the Hidden Truths of Tenure* (Chapel Hill: University of North Carolina Press, 2016).

The communications service saturated the public image with our presence. My colleagues and I appeared in brochures. Our portraits were on view in the entrance hall of the library. Thanks to us, the college boosted its prestige. On several occasions, a photographer showed up in class to take pictures—for what purpose, I did not know. One day, much to my astonishment, I found that I was featured on the home page of the college website.

The optical illusion camouflages a persistent invisibility. By exhibiting the Asian, Latinx, and Black students, the university obscures the fact that the majority of the professor and student body is white. Our over-representation on advertising platforms and social networks masks our under-representation in the institution. The over-exposure is window dressing. My status as a minority professor grants me marginal value. It is the guarantee of a random mobility that often compels me to negotiate my freedom with the compulsory figures of the white world. In spite of the historical, social, and economic particularities of my specific background, in the United States I define myself as a Black woman. Skin color forces me to deconstruct Black identity in the hierarchical and conflictual social sphere inherent to the country where I have chosen to live.

CHAPTER 2

Shades of Black

ADOS versus Black Non-descendants of American Slavery

When one says "Negro people," one systematically assumes that all Negroes agree on certain things, that they share a principle of communion. The truth is that there is nothing, a priori, to warrant the assumption that such a thing as a Negro people exists. [...] But when someone talks to me about that "Negro people," I try to understand what is meant. Then, unfortunately, I understand that there is in this a source of conflicts. Then I try to destroy this source.

Frantz Fanon, *Toward the African Revolution*[1]

We are living at a time when social networks are bombarded with a free flow of information and disinformation, ideologies, and conspiracy theories. At the same time, YouTube has become a platform for the emergence of an alternative, transgressive discourse on the Black condition in the United States. Opinion leaders such as Yvette Carnell, Antonio Moore, Meeche X, Professor Black Truth,

---

1 Frantz Fanon, *Toward the African Revolution: Political Essays* (Haakon Chevalier trans.) (New York: Grove Press, 1967), pp. 17–18.

Jason Black, and Tariq Nasheed have become active, influential voices on what has come to be known as Black Media. These eloquent speakers address an audience of Black Americans who listen to them two to three times a week. Showing themselves to be particularly critical of the Democratic Party that takes the Black vote for granted, they have raised a racial and ethnic consciousness that is different from the one established by earlier generations. They informed all the democratic candidates for the 2020 presidential election that without a political plan to meet the specific needs and interests of the African American community, the latter would not vote for them.

The proliferation of a novel type of discourse on social networks and YouTube invites us to reflect on the way in which the usual, politically correct channels of communication have contributed to creating, spreading, and solidifying analyses of the Black condition that no longer correspond to the expectations and experience of Black individuals. In the last twenty years, we have seen a series of concepts develop that, while referring to race, actually efface the uniqueness of the African American experience. Terms such as diversity, inclusion, equity, and minority belong to the prevailing newspeak which envisages race from the standpoint of integration and dilution in the white-supremacist power structure. The point is to generate opportunities of upward social mobility for non-white individuals in a fundamentally unequal system.

Substituting diversity for race creates a competition between Black Americans whose ancestors were slaves and Blacks who immigrated or whose parents immigrated voluntarily. The policies favoring diversity result from the struggle of descendants of slaves for freedom, equality, and social justice, but they have altered the

racial paradigm. African Americans have become just one component among many others in a rainbow of ethnic minorities. It is no
longer a question of examining the specificity of their historic condition so as to propose customized solutions but, rather, of obliter-
ating it. The fact is the historic condition and the current social
status of descendants of slaves does not correspond to the situation
of the Black people of voluntary-immigration origin.

Aware of this distinction and outraged by what they deem to
be the replacement of the African American population by another
from the Caribbean and sub-Saharan Africa, Yvette Carnell and
Antonio Moore propose a reconfiguration of the political discourse
from the standpoint of Americans who are descendants of slaves.
Their weekly YouTube broadcasts[2] have won them a loyal following.
Carnell and Moore created #ADOS: American Descendant of
Slavery.[3] The ADOS acronym distinguishes Black people whose
ancestors were reduced to slavery in the United States from those
originating in the Caribbean or sub-Saharan Africa. The economic
issue is at the core of Carnell's and Moore's concerns. Informed by
a series of statistical studies and research by economist William A.
Darity,[4] the two activists focus on the cause-and-effect relationship
between past slavery and racial segregation and the relegation of
ADOS to the very bottom of the social ladder. ADOS received no

---

2 Yvette Carnell, "Breaking Brown: Continuing the Tradition of Black Intellectual
Thought," available at: https://bit.ly/2XXFIfi; Antonio Moore, "Tonetalks," available at: https://bit.ly/3kJDgmk (both last accessed on August 13, 2020).

3 See "#ADOS Explained." Available at: https://ados101.com (last accessed on
November 25, 2020).

4 William A. Darity Jr. and A. Kirsten Mullen, *From Here to Equality: Reparations
for Black Americans in the Twenty-First Century* (Chapel Hill: University of North
Carolina Press, 2020).

compensation for the crime against humanity perpetrated against their ancestors.

The socioeconomic and historical observation made by Carnell and Moore is not new. Neither is the issue of reparations. Carnell, a former congressional aide, and Moore, an attorney, are situated at the periphery of recognized authorities in the academic and politico-media establishment. They have succeeded in imposing the debate on reparations in the public sphere.[5] No presidential candidate can ignore the question. Carnell and Moore argue that only reparations will reduce the huge income gap between white people and ADOS. Thus, the principle demand of the ADOS movement is for financial mechanisms to be established that will compensate ADOS for the unpaid work of their ancestors. While demanding a redistribution of wealth that will contribute to diminishing economic disparities between African Americans and whites, they conceive of social justice in terms of a nationally rooted genealogy. Because there is no reason that Black people whose ancestors were not enslaved in the United States should benefit from reparations.

The idea remains plausible that "there is an essentially modern Black condition and history that transcend the division between Africa and its diasporas and that are defined by structural overexposure to social and political violence and by the constant forced invention of survival strategies."[6] However, it merits qualification.

---

5 Farah Stockman, "Deciphering ADOS: A New Social Movement or Online Trolls?" *New York Times*, November 13, 2019. Available at: https://nyti.ms/-2VSTuyC (last accessed on December 8, 2020).

6 Norman Ajari, *La dignité ou la mort* (Les Empêcheurs de Penser en Rond; Paris: La Découverte, 2019), p. 10.

The ADOS movement asserts the specificity of their situation and contests the idea of a global Black condition. The use of the term diaspora refers to populations scattered from their indigenous lands by force or by choice. From a descriptive perspective, this term denotes an existential and historical situation. Although the Black diaspora has always been fragmented, the very concept of such a diaspora served the formation of an imaginary community. Today, Black populations in America are descendants of slaves (born in the United States or in the Caribbean) or descendants of the colonized (originating in sub-Saharan and East Africa). In spite of the fact that these different groups share the Black condition, they each occupy a distinct position in American society.[7]

The way in which Black populations in America think about identity and race is shaped by the history and culture of their country of origin. The separation established between the groups and the focus on lineage leads to a system of classification. The process of identity differentiation—ADOS versus non-descendants of American slavery—sheds new light on the relationship between race and historicity, race and ethnicity, race and social success. Race erases many factors that constitute the history of a person or determine her behavior in a given situation. Carnell and Moore insist on genealogy to delimit a family whose members come from an African population reduced to slavery in the United States. The two militants reproach those of sub-Saharan and Afro-Caribbean origin for their lack of deference toward ADOS and often use virulent language against them. For their part, non-ADOS are not exempt from criticism. Whether they were born in the United

---

7 Tod G. Hamilton, *Immigration and the Remaking of Black America* (New York: Russell Sage Foundation, 2019).

States, or arrived as children or adults, they sometimes demonstrate disdain toward African Americans. At the same time, they benefit from opportunities that arose from the ADOS struggle for civil rights. Without the long tradition of fighting for the freedom of Blacks, Afro-Caribbeans and sub-Saharans would never have come to the United States. The American dream would have remained the private property of whites.

The success of the newcomers goes hand in hand with the establishment of an identity distance between ADOS and non-descendants of American slavery. The pride felt for the land of one's ancestors and the identification with the culture of origin, as legitimate as they may be, often turn into an impassable wall designed to separate those of Afro-Caribbean and sub-Saharan origin from ADOS. Whether they are American citizens or not, Sub-Saharans and Afro-Caribbeans do not like to be conflated with African Americans.[8] Identitarian specificity acts as a shield against racial classification. Black non-descendants of American slavery of Afro-Caribbean or sub-Saharan origin do not want to adopt the heavy baggage attached to the African American identity. Their imaginaries are filled with embroidered memories, the heartbreaks of absence and of having to leave fragments of themselves far away. Pride is often the dominant note when we speak of our native countries. Positive adjectives abound. Every time an immigrant evokes the greatness of her native country, I wonder . . . If everything was so wonderful there, why are we here? Who are we fooling? Doesn't

---

8 The tensions and lack of understanding between Africans, Afro–West Indians, and African Americans are not new. Already in 1967, Harold Cruse discussed this situation in a chapter titled "Ideology in Black: African, Afro-American, Afro West-Indian and the Nationalist Mood," in *The Crisis of the Negro Intellectual from Its Origins to the Present* (New York: William Morrow, 1967).

our purported success in America hide our failures in Africa and in the Caribbean? The attachment and identification with the culture of origin acts as a mechanism of self-preservation and defense that protects the interiority of sub-Saharans and Afro-Caribbeans. It is a process of adapting and of rejecting the racial history of the country where we live.

Despite the color of our skin and the racism of which we too are victims, we refuse to don the historic livery. For ADOS, America, oppression, racism, and the fight for social justice are inseparable; for Afro-Caribbean and sub-Saharan immigrants, this country represents a land of possibilities. With sorrow slung over our shoulders and dreams within hope's reach, we left everything behind to live here. For all our identitarian bravado, when we fill out forms for grants, jobs, and advantages as a minority, we check the Black or African American box. No one claims a category with a reference to the country of origin. When a police officer shoots a Black person of sub-Saharan or Afro-Caribbean origin at point-blank range, the identity specificity vanishes. This violence does not happen only to ADOS. The officer did not kill a Jamaican, a Guinean, or a Haitian. He eliminated a nigger. Consequently, race and racism become the key modality of existence.

Police brutality reminds us that America is a white-supremacist state. As an armed instrument of the state, the police force disrupts the life of the Black individual without due process. Whether we accept it or not, the color of our skin lodges us de facto in the racial history of the United States. It situates us in it either as potential beneficiaries of preferential policies toward minority social groups that suffered from discrimination in the United States or as the main targets of police violence. To be sure, the murder of Black people by the police testifies to the most extreme aspect of state racism, but it is accompanied by numerous forms of direct or insidious racism to which Blacks are subjected in their everyday lives when it comes to work, health, and housing. Media attention focused on the success of Black non-descendants of American slavery masks the economic disparities inherent in a heterogeneous group. Sudanese, Somalian, or Eritrean refugees and Nigerian immigrants do not belong to the same social class.[9] A sizeable portion of newly arrived immigrants of sub-Saharan origin live below the poverty threshold.[10]

Populations originating in the Caribbean or sub-Saharan Africa carry a different existential baggage than ADOS. In their native countries, they were mainly confronted with problems of class, not race.[11] Despite neocolonialism and the post-colonial chaos, the face of power there is not white. In some Caribbean nations, it can be of mixed race due to the relationship between colorism[12] and class conflict. ADOS, on the other hand, have never

----

9 Whereas 59 percent of immigrants from Nigeria have a bachelor's or advanced degree, 10 percent of Somalian immigrants have reached a similar level of education. See Monica Anderson and Gustavo López, "Key Facts about Black Immigrants in the U.S." Pew Research Center, January 24, 2018. Available at: https://pewrsr.ch/30QDwrT (last accessed on August 13, 2020).

10 Poverty levels are highest in Somali and Liberian populations. See Carlos Echeverria-Estrada and Jeanne Batalova, "Sub-Saharan African Immigrants in the United States," Migration Policy Institute, November 6, 2019. Available at: https://bit.ly/3iE9LAQ (last accessed on August 13, 2020).

11 Except in the case of refugees of war and minority groups who were victims of genocide.

12 White supremacy established a system of racial classification in which Black people with light skin were more valuable and regarded as more attractive than those with a darker complexion. Unlike the slaves working in the field, domestic slaves were often mixed and could belong to the master's family. After

shed their status as a marginalized and dehumanized minority. The sociohistoric circumstances of Black populations in the United States conditions their psychological construction. Racism and the relationship to the white other does not affect ADOS and those of immigrant origin in exactly the same way.

Grappling with the heritage of traumatic violence (both physical and mental), exploitation, segregation, and dehumanization, whites and ADOS coexist in a conflictual relational space. The absence of a historical bone of contention between whites and Blacks of immigrant origin puts these two groups into a comfort zone. Between them there are no raped bodies, no mountains of corpses, no rivers of blood, or no chained memories. In a way, they share the immigrant experience and the search for the American dream. For this reason, it is easier to form ties that seem devoid of racism. The focus on the social success of populations of Caribbean and African origin reflects their capacity for integration in the space of the dominant. And this authorizes the latter to have a clean conscience.

The myth of the successful individual disregards the question of historicity. It ignores the fact that people are always situated—in many respects—and that this influences their perceptions and their discourse. Social success is an appealing mask that the white-supremacist system displays to deny and dissimulate the responsibilities of the American nation toward ADOS. In 2004, Sara Rimer and Karen W. Arenson published an article in the *New York Times* that broke down the admissions statistics of Black students to

---

the abolition of slavery, they formed a ruling caste. Colorism also manifests itself in interpersonal relations amongst kin, as individuals with darker skin can be the butt of insults and discrimination within their family.

the top American universities. The journalists cite Lani Guiner, a Harvard law professor, and Henry Louis Gates Jr., chairman of African and African American Studies at Harvard, who noted that two-thirds of Black students are Afro-Caribbean or African immigrants, or their children, or the children of biracial couples.[13] Thirteen years after the publication of this article, African American students at Cornell University protested against the over-representation of Afro-Caribbeans and sub-Saharans in the student population. They demanded that the university establish priority admission criteria based on lineage.

Affirmative action, designed initially for descendants of slaves whose social and economic advancement was obstructed by systemic racism, now benefits non-descendants of American slavery. The racial postulate at work in preferential admissions perpetuates the inequalities that it should have remedied. Access to higher education remains difficult for ADOS who represent only a third of Black students. Racial statistics paint a misleading picture that does not reflect the fragmentations and inequalities intrinsic to this group of people.

Blacks—no matter their origin—are interchangeable in a white-supremacist world in which the terms "minority" and "diversity" have been transformed into inclusive categories. Paradoxically, the triad *minority-diversity-inclusion* creates conditions favorable to the marginalization of ADOS. In 2018, the Pew Research Center reported that 69 percent of the sub-Saharan immigrant population in the United States had some college education. That is

---

13 Sara Rimer and Karen W. Arenson, "Top Colleges Take More Blacks, but Which Ones?" *New York Times*, June 24, 2004. Available at: https://nyti.ms/3iA14r2 (last accessed on August 13, 2020).

6 percentage points higher than white Americans whose ancestors immigrated starting in the seventeenth century and much higher than the education level of sub-Saharans in Europe.[14] Black populations of immigrant origin are better educated than ADOS.[15] A more specific study found that Nigerians transcend racial and ethnic criteria. They are one of the groups with the most degrees and their median household income is 62,351 dollars compared with the national average of 57,617 dollars.[16] These days, ADOS bear the costs of comparisons with immigrants from the Caribbean and sub-Saharan Africa and their descendants. Fifty years ago, the success of Jews, Italians, and Irish was used to deny the experience of descendants of slaves. Representatives of white power would bring up these European populations as proof that their initial marginalization did not keep them from succeeding. The conclusion was that African Americans were responsible for their own failure. Martin Luther King Jr. had this to say in response to such comparisons:

> Negroes were brought here in chains long before the Irish decided *voluntarily* to leave Ireland or the Italians thought of leaving Italy. Some Jews may have left their homes in Europe involuntarily, but they were not in chains when

---

14 Salem Salomon, "Study Finds Africans among Best Educated US Immigrants," Voice of America, April 24, 2018. Available at: https://bit.ly/-31Lw4gY (last accessed on August 13, 2020).

15 Monica Anderson, "Statistical Portrait of U.S. Black Immigrant Population," Chapter 1 of *A Rising Share of the U.S. Black Population Is Foreign Born*, Pew Research Center: Social & Demographic Trends, April 9, 2015. Available at: https://pewrsr.ch/3kGvEky (last accessed on August 13, 2020).

16 Molly Fosco, "The Most Successful Ethnic Group in the U.S. May Surprise You," *Ozy*, June 7, 2018. Available at: https://bit.ly/2FcnvnJ (last accessed on August 13, 2020).

they arrived on these shores. Other immigrant groups came to America with language and economic handicaps, but not with the stigma of color. Above all, no other ethnic group has been slave on American soil, and no other group has had its family structure deliberately torn apart. This is the rub.[17]

By establishing a relationship between race and oppression in a white-supremacist society, King describes the uniqueness of the African American condition. He also distinguishes between ethnic stigmatization and racial discrimination. Italians, Irish, and Jews may well have been considered distinct races, inferior to the white Anglo-Saxon Protestant population, but over time and thanks to targeted policies—white workers' unions, the New Deal, access to home loans—they were assimilated into the dominant white caste. Their native languages disappeared in most cases, even as these European populations held on to their cultural traditions.

The fable of the American melting pot would have us believe in the idea of a harmonious fusion between newcomers and the dominant white caste. But, as Toni Morrison observed, if America is indeed a melting pot, then Black people are the pot.[18] The low political, social, and economic status of African Americans is what made the mixing and assimilation of the various currents of European immigration possible. For several centuries, Asian, Chinese, and Japanese populations faced integration difficulties since they were not eligible to apply for American citizenship. This

17 Martin Luther King Jr., *Where Do We Go from Here: Chaos or Community?* (Boston: Beacon Press, 2010), p. 110.

18 *Toni Morrison: The Pieces I Am*, directed by Timothy Greenfield-Sanders, DVD (New York: Magnolia Pictures, 2019).

political exclusion facilitated the internment of Japanese in camps during the World War II. The marginalization of non-white immigrant populations was founded on the racial division opposing whites and Blacks. The discriminations that Asian populations experienced did not proceed simply from hatred or some irrational fear. It was a matter of maintaining a society built on racial division, white privilege, and the marginalization of people of color. Faced with rising immigration and the demographic change, President Donald Trump expressed the desire to abolish birthright citizenship. He went on the call for a reduction of immigration from "shithole countries" in particular, while encouraging European immigration from countries like Norway—thus perpetuating a discriminating ideology that targets only non-white populations from foreign countries.

At the time that King drew the distinction between the situation of African Americans and that of European immigrants, Black populations from the Caribbean and sub-Saharan Africa did not have considerable demographic weight in America. In 1990, George H. W. Bush's immigration reforms, particularly the Diversity Immigrant Visa, also known as the Green Card lottery, allowed residents from countries with a low rate of immigration to the United States to apply for a Green Card. The initial aim of the program was to diversify the immigrant population. Between 2005 and 2014, 46 percent of lottery winners came from Africa.[19]

When you immigrate to the United States, whether you're white or Black, you enter a racist social system. White immigrants

---

19 Ryan Struyk, "The Evolution of the Diversity Visa Lottery Program, in Charts," CNN, November 2, 2017. Available at: https://cnn.it/3kFJQKI (last accessed on August 13, 2020).

inherit the privileges historically attached to their race.[20] Their words are those of an individual. Their children receive an education that values their belonging to a racial group that does not define itself as such. They are presumed innocent, intelligent, and well brought up. Never would they be accused without proof of raping a jogger in Central Park. Whites are represented in the arts and in literature. They do not have to justify or excuse their presence. They embody success and power. Whites can criticize the politics of the United States without anybody telling them they should go back to the country they came from. Never will they be victims of redlining, the discriminatory practice of limiting or refusing mortgage loans to Blacks living in Black neighborhoods. Although the institutions have been designed to serve and protect their interests, whites will adamantly maintain that racism is the work of a stupid and intolerant minority, and in no case is it institutional. Whether Black individuals accept it or not, they are incarcerated in a sub-humanity perceived as inherent to the color of their skin. Depending on their family and historical roots, this heritage will not yield the same consequences.

More than once, I have found myself held hostage to conversations in which my personal, academic, and professional career path aroused astonishment, admiration, and curiosity. After six years in France, I had left my family for a country where I did not know a living soul. In spite of their gripes against the French, I found that Americans held French culture in high esteem. Not a week went by without someone speaking to me of the beauty of the language and the quality of French wine and food. I found myself

---

20 Peggy McIntosh, "White Privilege: Unpacking the Invisible Knapsack," *Peace & Freedom Magazine* (July–August 2009): 10–12.

invested with a collective heritage from which I could not disengage. My interlocutors associated me more readily with France than with Cameroon. After five years in the United States, I spoke English fluently, I had a PhD, and was starting my career in an Ivy League university on the East Coast. I gave the impression of having had a meteoric rise. I was the picture of the worthy immigrant, expecting everything from herself and never complaining.

Despite the economic difficulties and the racism that Black immigrants and their descendants have to confront, a sizeable number of them are beguiled by the fiction of the American dream.[21] A significant number of Afro-Caribbeans and Africans are seen as making the case for the American myth of success through hard work. Their life stories illustrate the national fable based on personal responsibility and individual initiative. The economic and social success of immigrants echoes American national values. These Blacks from elsewhere who work hard without asking anybody for anything embody triumphant America. They become exemplary figures of an American model in which meritocracy transcends race. Candace Owens saw fit to post a revealing tweet in this regard. Born to parents who came from the Virgin Islands, the Black figurehead of the Republican Party and supporter of President Trump pointed out that Nigerian Americans are the most prosperous ethnic group in the United States. Pitting "Blacks from underdeveloped Africa" against "Blacks from overprivileged America," she asserted that the former, not having been exposed

---

21 According to Tod G. Hamilton, "after residing in the United States for more than twenty years, black immigrant women from English-speaking Caribbean earn more than both black and white American women" (*Immigration and the Remaking of Black America*, p. 234).

to the Democratic discourse of victimhood, are able to accomplish in several decades what the latter should have been able to do after several centuries of presence on American soil.[22]

Shining a spotlight on the success of some Black people for the sake of blaming others for their failure works to project on the latter an image of losers. If America is racist, how is it possible that Nigerian Americans are thriving so soon after arriving here? This type of reasoning promotes the idea that African Americans are suffering from a deficiency that prevents them from taking advantage of what their country has to offer them. Republicans applaud the one group so as to humiliate the other. The argument of personal responsibility is used ad nauseam to deny the fact that enslaving human beings is wrong. Descendants of slaves deserve recognition and reparations for the physical, material, and moral harm caused by 245 years of captivity and forced labor, which were followed by Black Codes and the legal segregation that ended with the Civil Rights Act of 1964. Centuries of continual oppression led to the social and political marginalization of Black Americans. Sub-Saharan immigrants often come from West Africa, a region that was largely impacted by the transatlantic deportation.[23] They share the sub-Saharan roots of ADOS. But it is the association with whites and the intimacy established in an oppressive context that

22 @RealCadenceO, "Nigerian-Americans are the most successful ethnic group in the U.S! [...]" Twitter, July 4, 2019. Available at: https://bit.ly/2FovuOO (last accessed on August 14, 2020).

23 This expression was coined by Léonora Miano to shift the focus from the Western notion of "transatlantic slave trade" to one that emphasizes the story and point of view of the victim who was neither a slave nor Black but a human being forcibly enslaved and deported. See Léonora Miano, *L'impératif transgressif* (Paris: L'Arche Éditeur, 2016).

make descendants of slaves so different, so unmanageable and so incapable according to the system. It seems then that what is actually intolerable is the mirror held up to white Americans by the presence of ADOS. It reflects an image that brutalizes self-awareness.

As a consequence, African Americans occupy an odd place in society. The problems that confront them are regarded as ontological rather than historic or political. Something about the way that ADOS behave would be what makes them ill-suited for success. This ideological and revisionist sleight of hand has a double reach. On the one hand, the life stories of sub-Saharans and Afro-Caribbeans fits neatly into an American ethos that establishes a correlation between the immigrant experience and social success. On the other, to say that they are Blacks is meaningful only if one affirms that race has no negative impact on what becomes of them in America. The recognition is characterized by the absorption of sub-Saharans and Afro-Caribbeans into the national ethos of the American dream. They represent the narcissistic image of an America that achieves its dreams when Blacks are situated in a horizon of expectation required by the white-supremacist structure. While developing paradoxical forms of attachment, the politics of recognition serve the interests of the dominant.

The criteria authorizing recognition and validation are established by a state structure and a society whose egalitarian pretentions actually contribute to maintaining the dominant–dominated relationship. The absorption of a category of sub-Saharans and Afro-Caribbeans into the matrix of capitalist power adds to the vulnerability and precarity of ADOS.

Recognition of social success generates a fusion of same and other, and of racial and post-racial—the idea according to which race no longer stands as an obstacle to self-fulfillment. This alliance of opposites produces individual aberrations. Because these people define themselves and are defined as Black, they overuse the symbolic power of evocation. America has a voracious appetite for inspirational stories where the success of a handful of Black men and women blurs or abolishes the dichotomy between institutionalized racism and an apologia for social progress. Oprah Winfrey, Shawn Jay-Z Carter, Beyoncé Knowles, Sean Puffy Combs, Barack Obama, and the top basketball and American football players become figures exemplifying everyone's potential for success in a fundamentally inegalitarian society.

BARACK OBAMA: SYMBOLIC POWER OF EVOCATION AND DENIAL OF THE BLACK CONDITION

The essayist Ta-Nehisi Coates admits to an ambivalent relationship to Barack Obama's presidency. On the one hand, he recognizes that Obama did not handle the racial issue well. On the other, he insists on the powerful symbol represented by the country's first Black president.[24] To his mind, Obama contributed to enriching and diversifying the political imaginary by the mere fact of being the head of the government. The problem with this type of analysis is that it focuses on an individual whose main contribution is reduced to his capacity to inspire or spark enthusiasm. In short, Barack Obama made us dream. By exacerbating his symbolic power of evocation, an attempt was made to turn him into an antidote to the Black condition. The 2016 victory of Donald Trump, a white

---

24 Ta Nehisi-Coates, *We Were Eight Years in Power: An American Tragedy* (New York: Penguin Random House, 2017).

supremacist, testified to the contrary: a narrowing of the political imaginary and a return of the system whose death knoll was thought to have sounded with Obama's election.

Black politicians and celebrities are aporetic figures. In no way do they reflect the experiences of the majority of ADOS. Aware of the damage caused by the symbolic aura of this minority segment of the community, Carnell and Moore have denounced the politics of representation and visibility. The Huxtables in *The Cosby Show*, Barack Obama, Kamala Harris, and Oprah Winfrey are all anomalies. The promotion of the Black middle class leads to blindness, the inability to see the problems that the working class has to deal with, including access to quality education, the prison-industrial complex,[25] the breakdown of the family, school failure, violence, poverty, illness, poor-quality housing, and unemployment. The positive visibility of Black faces in high places encourages discourses on social success used to evade the structural issue.

The exceptional life stories of specific individuals should inspire the Black masses. And so racism is driven to the background, leaving self-determination and self-accomplishment front and center. But, like it or not, racism remains a political problem. The social success of a minority cannot cover up the situation of the majority.

25 "The prison-industrial complex is the result of a socioeconomic experiment conducted on three levels by the American government since the 1980s: the imprisoning, by means of ultra-repressive security laws, of a proportion of the population whose three main characteristics are being non-white, poor, and not integrated into a job market in which many jobs have been lost due to restructuration" (Laurent Laniel, "Le 'goulag américain'," available at: https://bit.ly/3aFYs8n; last accessed on August 19, 2020). Paradoxically, this system of mass repression intended to reduce the number of violent criminals has encouraged the mass incarceration of non-violent delinquents.

In response to the outrage over remarks by his pastor Jeremiah Wright, Obama gave a speech in which he used his personal biography as a starting point and an argumentative support for his thinking on racism. Raised by his maternal grandparents in Hawaii, Obama, the son of a Black man from Kenya and a white woman from Kansas, married Michelle LaVaughn Robinson, a descendant of slaves. His multiracial family is scattered across three continents. Draped in American exceptionalism, the idea that the United States has a particular destiny and unique role to play in the history of humanity, Obama argued that his life story could not have been possible anywhere else. In the speech, given on March 18, 2008 in Philadelphia, he portrays his pastor and his white grandmother—who sometimes gave voice to racist or ethnic stereotypes—as emblematic figures of his dual belonging to a country marked by racial division. These two people are part of America, the nation he cherishes.

Obama analyses racism in terms of his personal and sentimental drama. Lineage and family ties take the place of political arguments. By its affective thrust, the biographical narrative insists on anchoring identity in a way that relegates structural racism to the background. The racial issue takes on a private or relational dimension. On the basis of his supposed intimate familiarity with the white world through his maternal family and with the Black world through his wife's family and his pastor, Obama presents himself as an individual capable of transcending racial barriers. On the strength of a Black liberation theology that sees God as being on the side of the oppressed, Jeremiah Wright denounces systemic racism. Barack Obama, on the other hand, applauds the myth of racial and social progress.

When he tackles the racial issue, the president distills personal information and indulges in the dissemination of a subjectivity tinged with tenderness. He stresses the many emotional ties that culminate in a serene mix of different cultures. Yet he never speaks of himself as mixed-race. Yvette Carnell notes that when Obama defined himself as African American, the Black community celebrated the event with elation. The presidential candidate was simply doing a number on them but they took it as a sign of his identification with the experience of African Americans. Carnell appeals to the African American community to stop "looking for its reflection in President Obama. He may be the first [B]lack President, but he's certainly not the first African-American President."[26]

The racial system of identification was built on a eugenic premise whose purpose was to maintain the purity of the white race and the political oppression of Blacks. A drop of Black blood was enough to make you a descendent of slaves. Biracial individuals pose a problem for advocates of the ADOS cause, since the white parent, to their mind, gives the child access to privileges. Before the one drop rule was abrogated in 1967, it classified any person with one ancestor of sub-Saharan origin in a legal category that deprived them of rights reserved for whites. It did not matter that people of mixed-blood had a white parent or white ancestors; from a legal point of view, they were still Black. When their ancestry was not detectable, they would sometimes practice "passing." Whether or not they were biracial, in choosing to pass for white, they joined

---

26 Yvette Carnell, "Obama's Achilles Heel: He's Not African-American," *Huffington Post*, May 25, 2011. Available at: https://bit.ly/31anZmN (last accessed on August 19, 2020).

the dominant race to escape the Black condition and racism. Today they are often reproached for usurping a Black identity for personal gain.

Race eradicates the complexity of the human being for the purpose of justifying and reinforcing the dynamics of power between the dominant and the dominated. When a political figure publicly asserts a Black American identity, this positioning comes with obligations toward the community. Obama did not initiate an action plan addressing the socioeconomic problems of African Americans. Consequently, Carnell accuses him of playing the racial-identity card to win their votes. Knowing the capital of sympathy that his symbolic power of evocation gives him, Carnell draws a distinction between a "[B]lack President" and an "African-American President." The former is strictly descriptive and refers to skin color. The latter has to do with genealogy and refers to the historical, cultural, and political identity that characterizes ADOS—American Descendants of Slavery.

Barack Obama's election as president overturned racial schemas. Proof of the ability to transcend historical divides, the exceptional character of his life story was invested with a plurality of symbolic discourses: success through hard work, breaking the glass ceiling, America as a land where anything is possible, post-racial America, the exemplary Black family, etc. Americans elected a president who was Black, as we were continually reminded if only to assert thereafter that color was of no importance and could not be an obstacle to success. If this were true, then why harp on it? The reiteration of the discourse is needed to cast a spell over hearts and minds. It is the recitation of a mantra that acts like magical thinking, evacuating systemic racism without destroying it. Without having fundamentally transformed the oppressive society in which they live, the oppressed identify with this Black face, imagining that the doors to success are now open to one and all.

During his presidency, Barack Obama carefully avoided discussing the specificity of the Black condition in the United States and kept as much distance as possible from racial conflicts. When rioting erupted in Baltimore after Freddie Gray's death from injuries sustained in a police van, Obama called the rioters criminals. Although Martin Luther King Jr. advocated non-violence, when Blacks took to the streets of Detroit, Newark, Cincinnati, Buffalo, and Milwaukee, he observed that they did so to express anger and their desire for justice. Unlike the first Black president, King never employed *ad hominem* attacks. Without encouraging violence, King showed empathy and invited the American society and people in positions of authority to think about the meaning of these moments of collective revolt.[27]

Whereas King called on us to examine the conditions provoking the riots, Obama made use of vocabulary that resembles the racist jargon of ultra-conservative journalists and politicians. Throughout his terms in office, the first Black president seemed to have had a bone to pick with the Black condition. One of the most memorable instances illustrating this took place in May 2013, when the president gave a disconcertingly condescending speech at the

---

27 Martin Luther King Jr., "The Other America," speech delivered at Stanford University, California, April 14, 1967. Transcript available at: https://bit.ly/-34jtFwW (last accessed on August 20, 2020).

commencement ceremony at Morehouse College.[28] Founded in 1867, Morehouse College is one of the historically Black colleges and universities (HBCU) created for Blacks by Blacks and philanthropists and white missionaries at a time when descendants of slaves were excluded from the educational system.

One of the most elitist of the HBCUs, Morehouse College stands as a beacon of autonomy, resilience, courage, and the duty of excellence. It bespeaks the ethos of a population that takes its destiny into its own hands and refuses the limits that racist America imposes on it. The racial prison does not break the wings of freedom. Neither the historical context nor racism could defeat the educational project of the pioneers who founded this institution where Martin Luther King Jr., Spike Lee, and Samuel L. Jackson earned their degrees.

Commencement speeches coronate years of studies. They celebrate the achievements of the students while insisting on their duties to society. Here Obama was addressing a Black audience. He recognized the existence of racism. But his speech took an unexpected turn when, emphasizing his status as president of all Americans, he admonished his listeners. Obama began by maintaining that upward mobility concerns all Americans, regardless of race. Enlivening his speech with personal anecdotes, the American president admitted that when he was young he sometimes blamed

---

28 Today, HBCUs admit white students too. Their presence in some universities is changing the demographic composition. This new situation is provoking heated, conflictual debates. HBCUs are encountering multiple difficulties: a decrease in the number of graduates, competition with formerly all-white universities that are now accessible to all and funding problems. Out of a total of 107 HBCUs, 56 are private and 51 public.

his failures and his bad choices on whites. His criticism of the so-called culture of excuse took on outrageous proportions as he rattled off a litany of complaints: We've got no time for excuses, nobody cares if you've suffered some discrimination, nobody cares how tough your upbringing was.[29] If a white man had uttered such things, he would have been called all sorts of names.

Indeed, during his presidency, Obama treated Black Americans more as if he were a headmaster rather than a head of state. Under the sway of what he symbolized, enthralled by his charisma and feeling a sense of solidarity for a president who was the target of Republican racism, the Black community did not sound the alarm. Racism, discrimination, and the heritage of slavery produce a Black condition. The impact of these three existential markers has been proven—this Obama does not deny. Nonetheless, he imputes the consequences on bad personal choices. Racism is a problem from which Blacks should extricate themselves by making good decisions. The president summons his audience not to speak of institutional racism. He argues that resilience, transcendence, and inner courage can make the impossible possible.

The young men the president was addressing were not representative of the condition of Black males. Like Obama, the students at Morehouse College escaped prison, a lack of education, and premature death. Like the president to whom they listened attentively, they embodied the possibility of achieving personal success in a society that is hostile to them. This paradox is a reality that reinforces white supremacy. Submission to the implications of

---

29 Barack Obama, Commencement Address delivered at Morehouse College, Atlanta, Georgia, May 19, 2013. Transcript available at: https://bit.ly/3aG04Pz (last accessed on August 20, 2020).

this paradox has both whites and Blacks believing that class transcends race.

The Morehouse men chose to participate in a longstanding tradition rooted in the historical development of the community and the quest for its well-being. But they come from a group of individuals who are a minority and who also over-represented in negative statistics of incarceration, underperformance at school, unemployment, and poverty. This population is often obliged to examine its future through the prism of death.[30] The absurdity of a reasoning that shifts the focus from institutional racism to personal responsibility raises a fundamental question: What does the Black condition in imperialist democracies signify? Contrary to what they would have us believe, this condition is consubstantial with these societies, not external to them. In fact, it was spawned by these societies.

The republican discourse in France and the democratic promise in America were both perfectly compatible with slavery and colonization. The legacy of these two oppressive systems lives on, but when the oppressed bring it up, they are criticized for wallowing in victimhood: "an interpretation of oneself and the world as a series of fatalities"[31] stemming from the encounter with the West. They are expected to take themselves in hand and to bear on their frail shoulders the paralyzing consequences of 245 years of slavery followed by systems of segregation and alienation. Freedom is measured in terms of integration and assimilation to the world

---

30 Tommy J. Curry, *The Man-Not, Race, Class, Genre, and the Dilemmas of Black Manhood* (Philadelphia, PA: Temple University Press, 2017).

31 Achille Mbembe, "À propos des écritures africaines de soi," *Politique africaine* 77 (2000): 16–43; here, p. 25.

of the dominant. Instead of upsetting the established order and devising a transformative politics that would put an end to the resurgence of the world as it was, the focus is on living according to rules established by others.

If we examine the experience of Black Americans in light of democratic ideals, the idea of racial progress appears at best illusory and at worst delusional. Compare the income of the most under-privileged social classes: the average wealth of white families living near the poverty line is 18,000 dollars, while Black families in sim-ilar economic situations have a median negative net worth—that is to say, they are indebted.[32] The poorest sector of the white pop-ulation clings desperately to a sense of superiority that will never translate into hard cash. Capitalism elicits the need for there to be lowlier than oneself in order to accept one's unfavorable situation. Impoverished whites vote for Donald Trump and oppose the very governmental programs from which they could benefit. Statistics show that they are the first to profit from welfare. Yet the white-supremacist imaginary persists in maintaining that Black people are the ones living in a welfare culture. Ronald Reagan popularized the character of the "welfare queen" in repeated references to Linda Taylor, known for a series of criminal activities including welfare fraud. In political and media jargon, this pejorative term is used to refer to underprivileged Black women who are accused of fraudu-lently collecting excessive welfare payments. In 2016, the median

32 William Darity Jr., Darrick Hamilton, Mark Paul, Alan Aja, Anne Price, Antonio Moore, and Caterina Chiopris, "What We Get Wrong About Closing the Racial Wealth Gap," Samuel DuBois Cook Center on Social Equity at Duke University, Insight Center for Community Economic Development, April 2018. Available at: https://bit.ly/2FAMOA4 (last accessed on August 20, 2020).

wealth of a white household was 171,000 dollars, ten times higher than the average Black household.[33]

Between 1946 and 1994, Native Americans received 1.3 billion dollars as compensation, which amounted to the trivial sum of 1,000 dollars per person.[34] The country also recognized the damage inflicted on the Japanese during World War II. Under the Civil Liberties Act of 1988, the sum of 20,000 dollars was given to each survivor of wartime internment camps. The denial of the Black condition prompts unfortunate comparisons. But there is a need to explain that the poverty of Black individuals in the United States has deep-seated historical and structural causes that cannot be obscured by insisting on individual responsibility. After centuries of oppression, Black people demanded the right to live like other human beings. In 1969 James Brown wrote a song titled "I Don't Want Nobody to Give Me Nothing (Open Up the Door, I'll Get It Myself)." He was asserting his ability to take his life in his own hands, demanding only equal opportunity and quality schools to gain the tools needed to succeed in America. Fifty years after this song was released, the public-school system is still bankrupt, and equal opportunity is an ideal in which many people no longer believe.

Obama's eight years in the White House provoked a crisis of racial awareness that cannot be reduced to a strong resurgence of

---

33 Rakesh Kochhar and Anthony Cilluffo, "How Wealth Inequality Has Changed in the U.S. since the Great Recession, by Race, Ethnicity and Income," Pew Research Center, November 1, 2017. Available at: https://pewrsr.ch/3lbT6oS (last accessed on November 25, 2020).

34 Michael Lieder and Jake Page, *Wild Justice: The People of Geronimo vs. the United States* (New York: Random House, 1997), p. 257.

white supremacy. His terms were marked by an extreme visibility of police brutality, the emergence of the movement Black Lives Matter, and the killing of nine Black Americans in an African American church. After he won the presidential election in 2008, the symbolic impact triggered a phenomenon of mass identification around the world. In Europe, his resemblance to mixed-race Europeans was appreciated. On the African continent, his immediate ties with his paternal Kenyan family were felt all over sub-Saharan Africa: an African presided over the destiny of the world's leading power. His Indonesian childhood authorized a form of appropriation in Asia. Obama's appearance on the political stage had the effect of a cathartic drug that the American nation and the entire world needed. His campaign slogans—"Yes, we can!" "Change we can believe in"—carried a social and political ideal unanticipated during George W. Bush's terms in office.

After the 9/11 terrorist attack, President Bush urged his fellow Americans to go shopping, to take their families to Disneyland, and enjoy their lives. He dragged the country into an interminable war that began in Iraq and spread to several Middle Eastern countries. Obama's project for society stood in marked contrast with the consumerist and warmongering ideals of his predecessor. As soon as he became senator for Illinois, this soon-to-be-illustrious little-known figure hit the political stage like a blinding light, pulling America out of darkness and lifting the entire world to new heights of shared hope. From Chicago to Jakarta and from Paris to Nairobi, the entire planet was filled with joy.

Barack Obama dared speak of wealth redistribution in a country where many people think that the poor are poor because they choose to be. The symbolic impact went beyond skin color.

His lyrical speeches, full of compassion and informed by moderate optimism, moved people's imagination. During his first electoral campaign, he developed a political philosophy that, while uniting historically separate populations, emphasized that we were all soldiers of a revolutionary army, capable of creating a generous and just society. A few days after his election, I thought about the speech that he had delivered at the Northwestern University commencement. Sitting in the audience that day in June 2006, my classmates and I listened to the speaker inviting us to take risks, to persevere in the face of adversity, and to cultivate empathy for others. Barack Obama challenged us to change the world.

For certain minority groups, the president's deeds lived up to the ideals that brought him to prominence. He abrogated the policy that forced military personnel to conceal their homosexuality and came out in support of same-sex marriage after being against it for many years. Even though his government expelled a record number of undocumented immigrants, Obama signed the DACA (Deferred Action for Childhood Arrivals), a presidential decree granting legal status to immigrants who had arrived unlawfully in America when they were minors. For conservatives and the spokespeople of the ADOS movement, this was a gift to the Latinx community.

Arguing that he was president of all Americans, Obama refused to take initiatives that would have benefitted the Black community in particular. Instead of promoting concrete policies, he launched the My Brother's Keeper Alliance, a non-profit organization focused on mentoring young African American and Latino men. During his presidency, Black people were at the bottom of the social ladder in terms of wealth, employment, and home ownership.[35] The symbolic impact was losing momentum. Today, being Black does not suffice to ensure the unfailing support of the community. Kamala Harris learned this at her expense.

KAMALA HARRIS: BLACK IDENTITY AND POLITICAL OPPORTUNISM

A not-insignificant number of African Americans, who are very active on social networks and YouTube, have come to reject and denounce symbolic figures. Kamala Harris suffered the consequences thereof when she announced her candidacy for the 2020 presidential election. Black Media activists criticized her for her role as prosecutor in California in the mass incarceration of Black men and women. Given the disproportionate presence of African Americans behind bars, many argue that the fight against criminality is actually a war against Black people. Some will say that if Black individuals would just behave like good citizens, they would avoid prisons. Statistics show, however, that where the three-strikes law is concerned, Blacks are incarcerated twelve times more than whites. This law, or its various forms in twenty-eight US states, which allows judges to sentence offenders with two previous convictions to life in prison, applies to serious violent crimes or drugs offenses. However, petty criminals often find themselves imprisoned for life for minor offenses. The three-strikes law prevents any attempt at reintegration and rehabilitation.

---

35 Matt Bruenig and Ryan Cooper, "How Obama Destroyed Black Wealth," *Jacobin*, July 12, 2017. Available at: https://bit.ly/2YlaTRZ (last accessed on August 20, 2020). Eddie S. Glaude Jr., "President Obama and Black Liberals" in *Democracy in Black*: *How Race Still Enslaves the American Soul* (New York: Broadway Books, 2016), pp. 145–76.

By her very profession, Harris contributed to reinforcing a repressive system. As a candidate in the Democratic primaries, she declared she was in favor of legalizing marijuana; but when she was district attorney in California, she was strongly opposed to it and used the full force of law against such offenders. Harris presented herself as a progressive candidate; yet when she was prosecutor, she incomprehensibly refused to support body cameras on patrol officers.[36] Harris also established a program to prosecute parents whose children had an above-average unauthorized truancy rate. The charge carried the potential of fines up to 2,000 dollars and/or up to a year in jail. To prevent truancy and the illegal activities that result from it, Harris thought that she could save children from ending up on the streets by punishing their parents. Truancy rates fell by 40 percent. Parental responsibility is fundamental in the success of the young but punishing parents is also a way of infantilizing and undermining them when the aim is for them to demonstrate maturity and authority.

Given that 65 percent of African American families are single-parent households, a parent in jail or one who has become indebted to pay a fine cannot provide for their children. In cases when parents are vulnerable due to unemployment, mental illness, drug addiction, and homelessness, the situation is even more complicated. Talk of the living conditions of the underprivileged and people will rebuff you saying that you have to stop encouraging the culture of excuses. The fights and victories of the 1960s are often compared with the current decline. Such a perspective does not take into account the breakdown that contributed to fragmenting

---

36 Advocates of body cameras for police officers deem that it would help elucidate certain situations while reducing police violence and racial profiling.

the community. There was a time when the children of workers, doctors, and schoolteachers were neighbors; they went to the same schools and met every Sunday in church. Today, the Black middle class and the working class do not necessarily live together. Middle-class children attend private schools, while the others are trapped in school-zone policies that force students in difficulty to attend a school based on their address. Success or failure is determined by your zip code. The social diversity of the past facilitated a system of mutual aid that persists only marginally. Truancy is the symptom of a multifactorial social malaise. Instead of going after the parents, a better strategy would be to create mechanisms of intervention, enhance communication between schools and families, and see whether neighborhood associations and NGOs in problem areas can take over or at least serve as intermediaries to some extent.

To come back to Kamala Harris, she now regrets the criminalization of the parents of which she was the architect. Decriminalizing minor offenses, improving prisoner access to mental-health services, banning private prisons, and reforming bail procedures[37] were at the heart of the legal reform that she put forward to voters as a candidate for the Democratic primaries. In the eyes of supporters of the ADOS movement, Harris's past and her ideological

37 The bail system negatively impacts the poor who, for minor misdemeanors, are kept in jail where they can meet their death. In 2015 in Texas, Sandra Bland was incarcerated because she could not pay 500 dollars, 10 percent of the 5,000-dollar bail, needed to secure her release. Two days after her arrest, she was found hanging in her cell. The young woman had been stopped for a minor traffic violation which led to a violent interaction with the police officer. In 2019, Layleen Polanco, an Afro-Latinx transwoman, died in unexplained circumstances in Rikers Island Prison while being held in solitary confinement. After nearly two months in prison, she had not been able to raise the 500 dollars needed for her release.

positions before her candidacy belied the progressive image she was trying to project. Harris was accused of trying to take advantage of the Black electorate without really caring about its interests or well-being, just like Obama did. Without meaning to, the senator for California provoked a heated debate on identity and the question of reparations.

Born of a Jamaican father and an Indian mother—both university professors—Harris launched her presidential campaign in Howard University, a historically Black institution from which she graduated. She is also a member of Alpha Kapa Alpha, a Black sorority. Her candidacy was announced officially on Martin Luther King Jr.'s birthday. All these identity signals relayed to the African American community evinced her desire to be rooted in an African American cultural and memorial space? In an interview on *Breakfast Club*, a New York City–based hip hop radio show, Harris was questioned about her identity. "I'm Black, and I'm proud of being Black," she said. "I was born Black. I will die Black, and I'm not going to make excuses for anybody because they don't understand."[38] She also emphasized the diversity of populations in Black universities such as Morehouse, Spelman, Fisk, and Howard.

To be sure, there are Blacks of Caribbean and sub-Saharan origin in these institutions. But it was not from an Afro-diasporic perspective that Harris's identity was being questioned. No one was reproaching her for her genealogy. We choose neither our race nor the circumstances of our birth. These are contingent existential factors. She was not being attacked for the color of her skin but,

38 The Breakfast Club, "Kamala Harris Talks 2020 Presidential Run, Legalizing Marijuana, Criminal Justice Reform + More," YouTube, February 11, 2019. Available at: https://bit.ly/2Eio6nF (last accessed on August 20, 2020).

rather, for her ideological stance. Harris supported policies based on class that would benefit ADOS by default. But she overtly declared that she would not adopt measures to benefit Black people specifically.[39] At the same time, she advocated immigration policies that would allow undocumented young adults to be regularized. She was also working on legislation to give the parents of American children who had entered the United States illegally a way to get Green Cards. Like Obama, she only opposed particular interests when it came to Black Americans. She played the racial card for her personal interests. Her communication staff shared a video of her dancing to Cardi B. In her *Breakfast Club* interview, she also confessed that she had smoked marijuana while listening to 2Pac and Snoop Dogg. While Obama admittedly charmed a great many people by singing Al Green or dancing to Etta James with his wife, Harris's appeal to the Black community were stereotypical and bordered on the grotesque.

Due to a lack of funds, the senator ended up dropping out of the Democratic primary race. Then Biden, despite her violent attacks on his past positions on racial segregation policies, not to mention his connections with racist senators, chose her as his running mate. Four months earlier, the *Washington Post* posted an opinion video by LaTosha Brown, Tiffany D. Cross, Brittany Packnett Cunningham, Alicia Garza, Sunny Hostin, Angela Ryes, and Amanda Seales urging Joe Biden to choose a Black woman as vice president.[40] In the wake of the wave of protests against racism

---

39 theGrio, "#AskKamala: Does Kamala Harris Support Reparations for Black Americans?" YouTube, February 24, 2019. Available at: https://bit.ly/2Qc4pjS (last accessed on August 20, 2020).

40 LaTosha Brown, Tiffany D. Cross, Brittany Packnett Cunningham, Alicia Garza, Sunny Hostin, Angela Rye and Amanda Seales, "Biden Still Needs Black

and police brutality that marked the summer of 2020, Harris's nomination was seen as a strong signal. In the weeks leading up to the elections, opinion polls disputed the stereotypes about voter profiles. It turned out that support for Donald Trump was growing among Black men. The rapper Ice Cube, after fruitless attempts to communicate with the Democratic Party, presented the Republican candidate's campaign with a proposal for an agenda for Black Americans.[41] The rapper was excoriated on social media by the cohort of Blacks who police what other Blacks should think and do. Rappers Lil Wayne and 50 Cent publicly expressed support for Donald Trump, which outraged these right-thinking moralists.

In reaction to the emergence of these transgressive, dissident voices, Brittney Cooper, a Black feminist, professor of gender and women's studies, argued that Trump's toxic masculinity corresponded to the male archetype in hip hop culture. Without mincing words, she maintained that Black men wanted to be patriarchs and male-dominant in the way white men are.[42] Jumping on Cooper's bandwagon, the journalist Jemele Hill sent out an accusatory tweet: "Black men just want better access to patriarchy. They don't actually want it dismantled."[43] The idea that Black men who voted for

---

Women. Here Are 3 Things He Needs to Do," *Washington Post*, May 14, 2020. Available at: https://wapo.st/378YdRZ (last accessed on November 25, 2020).

41 Ice Cube, "A Contract with Black America." Available at: https://contractwith-blackamerica.us/ (last accessed on November 25, 2020).

42 Jonathan Capehart, "The 'Eloquent Rage' of Brittney Cooper over Black Men Voting for Trump," *Washington Post*, October 21, 2020. Available at: https://-wapo.st/3l1BxYI (last accessed on November 25, 2020).

43 Janice Williams, "Jemele Hill Claims 'Black Men Just Want Better Access to Patriarchy' and People Aren't Happy," *Newsweek*, October 20, 2020. Available at: https://bit.ly/365pkOf (last accessed on November 25, 2020).

Donald Trump may not all be misogynous and aspire to patriarchal privilege is simply unthinkable. Yet some of these voters agreed with the Republican candidate's discourse, while others were intent on penalizing the Democratic Party for considering them a captured electorate. Didn't Biden say to radio presenter Charlamagne tha God that if you have a problem choosing between Trump and him, then "you ain't Black"?[44] Biden has yet to atone for his memorable diatribe against Black men, calling them predators and sociopaths who cannot be rehabilitated and must be taken out of society.[45] The ideological activism of Brittney Cooper and Jemele Hill, dressed in dogmatic anti-Trumpism peppered with radical feminism, reduces issues of gender, race, and sexuality to antagonisms, ultimately culminating in an intra-community war between Black women and Black men.

During the summer of 2020, the Democratic presidential candidates showed compassion and empathy toward those who lost loved ones to police violence. But where was this fine humanism in 1994, when Joe Biden, architect of the Violent Crime Control and Law Enforcement Act, inaugurated a period of mass incarceration and racial disparities in the criminal justice system?[46] Where was the concern for victims when Kamala Harris was   attorney general

---

44 C ThaGod, "Joe Biden On Dems Owing the Black Community, Criticism of the 94 Crime Bill, Health Issues + More," YouTube, May 22, 2020. Available at: https://bit.ly/3m9Lepd (last accessed on November 25, 2020).

45 Joe Biden's speech in the US Senate, November 18, 1993. Available at: https://cnn.it/3m9VuOe (last accessed on November 25, 2020).

46 See Michelle Alexander, *The New Jim Crow: Mass Incarceration in the Age of Colorblindness* (New York: New Press, 2012).

in California?[47] President Biden and Vice President Harris refuse to own their implication in the prison-industrial complex that mainly targets Black men. The point is not to prosecute the new executive duo for their past track record. To err is human. But the people who paid the consequences thereof deserve to be recognized publicly and to receive tangible reparations that will help undo decades of institutional injustice.

The witch-hunt against Black male voters evidences the tyranny of consensus that considers that minorities have an obligation to vote for the Democratic Party. In the end, 18 percent of Black men voted for Donald Trump and Mike Pence, while 82 percent opted for Joe Biden and Kamala Harris. In 2016, 4 percent of Black women chose Donald Trump over Hilary Clinton. Four years later, the percentage of this electorate that voted for the incumbent president doubled, despite the fact that a Black woman was on the Democratic ticket.[48] And instead of reflecting on a new electoral reality that complicates the interrelationship between race and identity,[49] we have binary simplifications. On the one hand, Black women are deified for saving the country from destruction

47 See Lara Bazelon, "Kamala Harris Was Not a 'Progressive Prosecutor'," *New York Times*, January 17, 2019. Available at: https://nyti.ms/378xzbU (last accessed on November 25, 2020).

48 See Jacob Jarvis, "Donald Trump Made Gains in Every Demographic Except for White Men," *Newsweek*, November 5, 2020. Available at: https://bit.ly/-3o2BT3f (last accessed on November 25, 2020).

49 In the Hispanic community, 36 percent of the men and 32 percent of the women voted for Donald Trump. See, among others, Christine Zhang and John Burn-Murdoch, "By Numbers: How the US Voted in 2020," *Financial Times*, November 7, 2020. Available at: https://on.ft.com/2HDCMzH (last accessed on November 25, 2020).

by massively voting for the Democratic Party.[50] On the other, Black men are demonized for voting against the Democrats. With this obsessive attention paid to the minority that identified with Trump, the majority without which Biden could not have won the election is dismissed out of hand. Such a skewed representation promotes the idea of Black female exceptionalism at the expense of the male population, reduced to the irrevocable common denominator of patriarchy and toxic masculinity.

In her first speech as vice president–elect, Kamala Harris paid tribute to the women "who fought and sacrificed so much for equality and liberty and justice for all, including the Black women who are too often overlooked but have so often proved they are the backbone of our democracy." Harris also said she was thinking about "the generation of women, Black women, Asian, white, Latina, Native American women who throughout our nation's history have paved the way for this moment."[51] Expressing gratitude to the generations that came before her, Harris positioned herself as heir to a long-standing struggle. The minority identity—gender and race—undergirding her words serves as a bargaining chip and a political category legitimating access and the right to power. Harris is the first woman and first Black person to be vice president of the United States. Some foresee the possibility of her becoming the next president. Without challenging the economic and political

50 Brittney Cooper, "Kamala Harris and Black Women Voters Helped Joe Biden Get Elected. Here's How America Can Do Right by Them," *Time*, November 8, 2020. Available at: https://bit.ly/3m95lUC (last accessed on November 25, 2020).

51 See Matt Stevens, "Read Kamala Harris's Vice President–Elect Acceptance Speech," *New York Times*, November 8, 2020. Available at: https://nyti.ms/-2V7y93K (last accessed on November 25, 2020).

structures that lead to the exclusion of women and people of color, asserting affiliation to a minority identity category maintains a confusion that is at once strategic and fallacious. The achievement of one individual is seen as fitting into a collective narrative in which everything becomes possible for the marginalized. The national imaginary and the jubilant public ascribe a magical power to these historical moments that inform a schizophrenic relationship to reality. A mythical construction purported to transcend structural inequities, the horizon of possibilities becomes infinite in a society strewn with obstacles and dead-ends. Like in a Hollywood movie, the happy ending magically wards off the social tragedies prevailing in disadvantaged Black communities: "While I may be the first woman in this office, I will not be the last, because every little girl watching tonight sees that this is a country of possibilities."[52]

Americans got rid of a dangerous, cynical, unpredictable president, the "neo-fascist gangster" Trump,[53] and with good reason. But a return to normalcy must not be conflated with some sort of radical transformation of the political superstructure. Biden and Harris are not proposing anything revolutionary. They are putting an end to a nightmarish populist period. The 2020 presidential election was a referendum against Donald Trump. The cathartic joy of Democratic voters celebrating victory and the powerless rage of Republicans refusing to accept defeat are the revolting trappings of a democracy in which identity-based emotion acts as a catalyst

---

52 Stevens, "Read Kamala Harris's Vice President–Elect Acceptance Speech."

53 Cornel West in Tonetalks, "Biden Set to Win Election 2020—Dr. Cornel West—Where Do We Go from Here with Voting?" YouTube, November 5, 2020. Available at: https://bit.ly/377KpHj (last accessed on November 25, 2020).

for a dystopian civic consciousness. James Baldwin rightly spoke about the peculiarities of a society obsessed with the first Black person being elected to the highest office in the country, when what he was especially curious about was what kind of country that person would be president of.[54] To this question we must now add a critical reflection on the symbolic power of evocation enjoyed by minority elites. In presuming that the skin color, gender, or sexual orientation of a person acceding to a high office fundamentally carries a progressive or redemptive political agenda, we are attributing questionable axiological properties to contingent identity characteristics. This way of apprehending existence fuels a process of collective delirium and blindness that is antithetical to liberation. We cannot help but recognize with some dismay that race, gender, and sexual orientation have become very important forms of symbolic capital for minority elites.

Harris's historic triumph, like Obama's, sublimates a hegemonic paradigm—that of capitalist democracy. Media outlets, intellectuals, and politicians would have us believe that integrating a handful of carefully selected representatives of minorities advances humankind. But this integration of an elite, with which the masses are supposed to identify, reflects the paradoxes of a white-supremacist society that obliterates the fragmentation of experiences of race, gender, and sexuality. Minorities that are part of the system never transform it, because they stand to benefit from it. There is in fact an alliance of converging interests between the democratic white middle class

---

54 James Baldwin, *The Cross of Redemption: Uncollected Writings* (Randall Kenan ed.) (New York: Vintage International, 2011), p. 9.

and the middle-class aspirations of minority elites.[55] Their upward mobility puts the masses to sleep. Instead of rebelling, they take vicarious pleasure in the success of others.

Asserting a Black identity once presupposed a political commitment grounded in a concern for improving the conditions of a community made up of those whom Eugene Robinson called the abandoned—that is, the population of American descendants of slaves who remain prisoners of poverty and despair.[56] The Blacks who are not descendants of American slavery were always engaged in political struggles.

Shirley Chisholm, whose parents hailed from Guyana and Barbados, was the first Black woman in Congress and the first Black candidate to seek nomination for president of the United States. She was a champion of education and employment for minorities. Harry Belafonte, the actor of Jamaican origin, played a very important role during the civil rights movement. The Trinidadian Stokely Carmichael was active by the side of Martin Luther King Jr. before joining the Black Panthers. Even though the number of Black non-descendants of American slavery has increased substantially, they remain a minority. In the 1960s and

---

55 See Robert Chrisman, "On Robert Allen's *Black Awakening in Capitalist America*: 'The Black Middle Class, Forty Years After',", *The Black Scholar* 40(2) (Summer 2010): 49–53.

56 According to Robinson, the vast "abandoned minority" stands apart from the elite whose access to wealth and power makes it possible for them to bridge the racial divide. The journalist also identifies two new groups: mixed race and recent Black immigrants. These groups, he argues, complicate the mode of comprehending and interpreting Black identity in the United States (Eugene Robinson, *Disintegration: The Splintering of Black America*, New York: Anchor Books, 2011).

'70s, these immigrants adopted the combat of African Americans. At the time, the solidarity between oppressed Black people crossed the continents. When certain journalists criticized Obama for not taking an interest in the specific situation of Black Americans, he declared that he was not the president of Black America.[57] Harris adopted the same attitude and contented herself with defining her identity based on her skin or on Afro-diasporic diversity. But this is not what is in question. When a journalist asked her if she defined herself as an Indian American, she replied that she was a proud American.[58]

Harris's critics do not oppose racial identity to citizenship. They denounce the use of a Black identity that ensures electoral legibility without making any tangible promises to the African American community. In defining herself, like Obama, as a Black American, she positions herself in a particular historical framework and becomes heir to the struggle of ADOS to the spheres of power from which they were excluded. Unlike the two politicians who are Black Americans born of one or two foreign parents, I am a naturalized citizen of the United States who arrived in this country as an adult immigrant. My presence in the academic system and the recognition of my area of research is situated in a continuity that is historically rooted in the struggles by African Americans for the creation of Black studies in the 1960s and '70s.

57 Barack Obama, interview by Derek T. Dingle, *Black Enterprise*, August 6, 2012. Available at: https://bit.ly/3lqRcRA (last accessed on December 1, 2020).

58 Gabriella Muñoz, "A Daughter of Immigrants, Kamala Harris Sees Herself as a 'Proud American'," *Washington Times*, January 21, 2019. Available at: https://bit.ly/2EabTBC (last accessed on August 20, 2020).

RESPONSIBILITY: ARE WE PART OF THE PROBLEM OR OF THE SOLUTION?

I'm a Black female immigrant and a professor of Africana studies, and I would be lying if I told you that I am constantly thinking of defeating white supremacy. The way that the human condition is expressed in sub-Saharan Africa and in the diaspora is at the heart of my academic preoccupations. The continuities and discontinuities between oppression and freedom have led me to an unshakeable conviction: Black people, wherever they are, have to take up the challenge of the future and be the light whose emergence from the darkness of servitude remains indispensable. The classes I give and the books and articles I write examine the perpetual struggles of populations of sub-Saharan origin for social justice and freedom. Some of the criticisms of ADOS are addressed to people with my profile. I am accused of usurping a place that is not mine. I could have lived in France or gone back to Cameroon.

Place of birth and race are givens that are out of our control. But they have been used to guarantee certain privileges so as to reject equality between individuals, deny the sacredness of the human being, and establish a will to power. If I were reproached for taking the place of an African American, I would not feel the need to justify myself. American universities are overflowing with professors of sub-Saharan and Afro-Caribbean origin. Instead of railing against their presence, the leaders of the ADOS movement should be asking about the quality of their teaching, the type of relationship that they have with African American students, and their degree of commitment to the fight against racism. If all these university professors would disappear, their departure would not contribute to the advancement of African Americans.

The success of sub-Saharan or Caribbean non-descendants of American slavery provokes righteous anger. With some resentment, Antonio Moore observes that Haitians in Miami have higher incomes than African Americans even though they come from one of the poorest countries in the Northern Hemisphere. Acknowledgement of downward social mobility goes hand in hand with the fundamental fear of being replaced by immigrants. All societies in crises have a need for a scapegoat. Now it is the new-comers that stand in the way of ADOS accomplishing their destiny. And so Black non-descendants of American slavery are reproached for a lack of involvement in the struggles of African Americans. We are thus regarded as the useful idiots of white supremacy. Things are not that simple. I live in a world where the present is but the future of a hidden past that shapes wounded minds.

The spring of 2015 marked a decisive turning point in my educational approach. A series of events shook the liberal arts college where I was teaching at the time. Over a period of about ten days, the college's president found herself having to respond to accusations of racism, anti-Semitism, and Islamophobia. A colleague posted a controversial message on Facebook that ultimately led him to take a sabbatical semester. An ill-chosen metaphor gave the impression that the professor had dehumanized an oppressed people. A pro-Palestinian group of students denounced him and he defended himself saying that he was referring only to Hamas. To no avail. He had started a fire. In an attempt to repair the damage, the president of the college gave an awkward speech on freedom of speech and the dangers of inciting racial hatred. A few days after this speech that served no purpose, someone had the brilliant idea of writing "No niggers here" in the restroom of a student building.

In the United States, "nigger" is not just any old word. When used by a white person, no matter the context, the term has an injurious connotation. When white people pronounce the word "nigger," it carries with it the memory of the violence that legitimated the subjection of Blacks and the negation of their humanity. The racist graffiti caused outrage. A group of students stormed the home of the college's president a stone throw from campus. They also spoke before TV cameras.

Classes were cancelled the day after the incident. Professors, students, and administrators participated in a series of debates on racism, inclusion, and equity. During these exchanges, some white students, with their antiracist bible in hand, slammed those in charge of the college. There were attendees who would have liked to speak their minds but hadn't the courage to do so. With attendance mandatory, most of the students confined themselves to occupying their assigned seats. That day, African Americans made themselves heard. With trembling voices, flushed with rage, tears sometimes streaming down their faces, they poured out their hearts about the many forms of exclusion they experienced in and out of the classroom. The question of racism did not worry me much. It was to be expected and you had to be ready to face it. After all, we were living in America. Forced to examine their humanity through the prism of multiple deficiencies, the African Americans who testified that day doubted their ability to succeed in a hostile environment. Yet they were, as the Nina Simone song says, "young, gifted, and Black." They were expecting the administration to pay

attention to them and take care of them. Something it was incapable of doing.

I recall with weariness the many meetings I was invited to. The
organizers of these gatherings spoke of students of color as if they
were dealing with unresolvable problems. Nothing was done to
enable these students to blossom as human beings. I discovered a
form of racism that I had not always been aware of. No one
demanded that Black students excel. They were expected to have
difficulties. Their failure only confirmed prejudices. And because
diversity is de rigueur, the college was delighted by their presence.

The way the administration responded to the incidents that
took place on campus evidenced crass ignorance tinged with arro-
gance. The governing bodies demonstrated a paternalistic, emotional
approach to the racial question. They invited students to tell their
personal stories. When confronted with the question of racism, the
most competent, well-educated people lost all ability to think crit-
ically. There we were in an institution that was giving them access
to a library, to professors, and to countless resources. But some subjects did not deserve to be taken seriously. All that was needed was
to hear the voice of the oppressed, people scarred by life for whom
one felt compassion without having to question the role one may
have played in their misfortune. Theirs were intimate difficulties.
They needed to be consoled or placed in the hands of the only Black
psychologist on campus, who found herself flooded with appoint-
ments. After a few weeks on campus, many of the Black or Latinx
students had panic attacks, sunk into depression, or became insom-
niacs, though they had been quite sane when they arrived.

The uproar in the spring of 2015 pulled me out of my routine.
I was giving most of my courses at the time in the language of

Molière. Only two of them were in English. One of these, open to first-year students, focused on the colonial experience; the other on LGBTQI issues in sub-Saharan Africa and the Caribbean. I attracted a limited number of students. After the incidents I had witnessed, I understood that the college was my community. I had to choose between being part of the problem or of the solution. It was not enough to lash out at racism and ignorance. I began to think of giving a course on the Black experience in the United States. That's how "Existence in Black" came into being. The course became a key component of the Africana studies program. I taught it every year from the spring of 2016 on. The course was premised on examining the infinite possibilities of human beings in the face of their destiny, on analyzing the ongoing tension between denouncing oppression and asserting one's capacity to act, on understanding that, in an imperialist democracy, freedom is never acquired once and for all—it has to be conquered again and again. It begins and persists in the fight against all that opposes it. The combat starts with the awareness that one has of oneself.

The students enrolled in "Existence in Black" were African, Afro-Caribbean, African American, Arab, Latinx, Asian, and American of European descent; they chose to take a course which was not a requirement for reasons of their own. The diversity in the class did not correspond to the college's. But it did reflect a world to come that is incumbent upon us to create. These students were majors in a variety of subjects: philosophy, economics, anthropology, psychology, Africana studies, sociology, dance, and American civilization. The fact that they came from different academic disciplines lent itself to rich, unconventional discussions.

The first time I gave the course, I noticed with amusement that a portion of the African American and Afro-Caribbean students had taken over the front of the classroom. This group of activists, whom I knew, wanted to mark their territory. The sometimes-lively discussions reproduced the dynamics of power in society. I remember a white student asking me if the depictions of events in the films *The Middle Passage*[59] and *Sankofa*[60] were accurate. Another declared that she did not understand the interest of studying Negro spirituals: "Why did these Blacks believe in a God that allowed slavery?" she asked. One student expressed his frustration that he could not simply enjoy the blues without dwelling on the existential dimension of the musical genre. He was one of so many people who appreciate Black music without worrying about the experience of the people who created it.

Exasperation could sometimes be read on the faces of the Black students who were trying to keep their irritation to themselves. To the consternation of some white students, this annoyance would explode at times. The Black students identified with the issues being discussed. The personal and intuitive knowledge they had of them came up against critical thinking. Their classmates' comments and questions often displayed unconscious racism, accompanied by a tendency to listen to themselves expatiate. The discordant episodes proved to be conducive to learning to live together. On several occasions, I had to contain my own annoyance and reframe what I was saying with patience, love, and comprehension.

59 *The Middle Passage*, directed by Guy Deslauriers, DVD (New York: HBO Home Video, 2003).

60 *Sankofa*, directed by Haile Gerima, DVD (Washington, DC: Mypheduh Films, 1993).

We discussed issues directly related to the situations and dilemmas plaguing Black people in America. One day, out of the blue, an African American student gave vent to a cold rage. The education he had received had not provided him after three years with the necessary tools to understand his existence. Most of the students had never been exposed to the authors and artists who were on the course syllabus. They were particularly moved to discover the likes of Nina Simone, Billie Holiday, James Baldwin, Lewis Gordon, Audrey Lorde, Marcus Garvey, W. E. B. Du Bois, Tommy J. Curry, and Kimberley Crenshaw. The names of Martin Luther King Jr. and Malcolm X were familiar to them. The young generation had memorized some of their quotations or wore t-shirts bearing their portraits without having studied their writings. The white students accepted to hear truths that struck blows to their ego at first. As time went by, the initial wound gave rise to a new self-awareness. Unlike the majority of whites, adept at denial and evasion, they had put themselves in danger and let themselves be shaken. The identification and disidentification with the figure of the persecutor or the victim influenced the process of reflection. The problems of analysis or of comprehension testified to the difficulty in recognizing what history had made of us while asserting our capacity to create a more just world.

Cinematic depictions of abduction, branding, rape, forced labor, and the social life of the oppressed have given a human face to a painful history that was often confined to overarching concepts such as the transatlantic slave trade and oppression which paralyzed thinking. In my many exchanges with students, I observed that the subject of the transatlantic slave trade limited thinking to two issues: the violence exercised by whites over Blacks and the lack of freedom. This approach does not take into consideration the sub-jectivity of the individual, trapped in a situation of extreme suffering. The words that human beings reduced to slavery speak about their experience are inaudible. They should however make us wonder about how it is that the universality of humanity, although widely recognized, is constantly confronted with a system of classification and domination. Transatlantic slavery trapped some in resentment or victimhood, and others in guilt or denial. There were those who went on and on about the Haitian revolution, forgetting that run-ning away and modes of passive revolt—such as the supposed lazi-ness of Blacks that the master complained about—had played an important role. Literature, cinema, and music gave the students a picture of the human experience that revealed the relationship between freedom and anxiety, improvisation and resistance, and the possibilities of faith in the face of doubt. The students discovered a previously unknown truth: Black people were not merely victims. By focusing on their oppression, one was effacing their social life.

Without any doubt, the privation of freedom conditions and limits the experience of a human being. Yet the individual remains a subject whose humanity is asserted by maintaining the bond with members of her community. The celebration of a birth, a marriage, funerals, religious practice, the oral transmission of myths and beliefs, conflicts, family relationships, love relations are all part of the life of Black people, be they prisoners on a plantation or victims of racial segregation. Students realized that we were dealing with individuals who were questioning the meaning and value of their lives. The reflection followed the meanders of a mind in a state of tension. The students, torn between their self-image and the image of the Black person's destiny, reassessed the racist framework that had shaped their understanding of Black identity and American history. In the end, the classroom became a space where people who crossed paths without meeting one another had to find a peaceful way to exist together. Now they had to spread the good word outside the classroom walls.

For a long time, I had objected to taking on administrative responsibilities, which did not exempt you from teaching but added to your work load. After the events in the spring of 2015, I decided to take on positions that would give me the possibility of testifying and also of disturbing the established order and influencing the racial climate on campus. I had to be integrated into places of power. I became the faculty advisor of a student organization against racism. I took the opportunity to chair the French department and directed the Center for the Critical Study of Race and Ethnicity (CCSRE).[61] Thanks to these new responsibilities, I was in a position to initiate discussions on controversial subjects, invite researchers and activists on campus, question the administration about its refusal to effect deep-seated structural changes, and support a Black colleague who was being harassed. The content of my teaching and the roles I chose to take on embedded me in an Africana intellectual tradition in which education and freedom are synonymous.

---

61 The center supports interdisciplinary research and teaching and artistic expressions that reflect the need for critical thinking across disciplines on race, ethnicity, and social differences (gender, class, sexuality, indigenous groups). We sponsored researchers, activists, and artists to come to campus, funded research by students and professors, and organized many initiatives around issues of inequality. We also established yearly partnerships with academic fields where minorities are underrepresented, notably in the sciences.

COME SUNDAY[62]

Unlike the immigrants who find in their compatriots the part of themselves they left behind, I never sought the company of French or Cameroonian people. Chance sometimes placed them on my path, in Chicago, Providence, or New Haven, but these encounters did not lead to friendships. My spiritual quest took me to the African American Baptist Church. The faith of people who chart their course starting from an impasse moved me deeply. In addition to the words heard and repeated Sunday after Sunday came the influence of Black American theologians like James H. Cone and Howard Thurman, without forgetting the contribution of Marcus Garvey.[63]

I came to understand that prayer was not a magical incantation that the believer utters hoping for an end to their woes. And so I constituted my daily breviary: "Please my Lord, I do not ask you to move my mountain, only to give me the strength to climb it. I do not ask you to calm the storm, only to bless my spirit with the endurance needed to pass through it. Unspeakable joy overcomes sadness. All is grace. Misfortune does not crush the believer, it strengthens her. Regardless of human vicissitudes, life is a miracle. Honoring God means refusing captivity and fatality by becoming master of your destiny."

---

62 Duke Ellington and His Orchestra, featuring Mahalia Jackson, "Part IV" (aka "Come Sunday") in *Black Brown & Beige*, CD (New York: Columbia Records, 1999).

63 Marcus Garvey, "The Resurrection of the Negro" in *Selected Writing and Speeches of Marcus Garvey* (Bob Blaisdell ed.) (New York: Dover Thrift Editions, 2005), pp. 66–69.

Moved by preaching that breaks chains, enthralled by music whose cathartic virtues brought peace in the face of tribulations, sensitive to the kind generosity of people who did not know me, I felt welcome and safe. In an unexpected transformation, I set the abstract Catholicism of my childhood and my years of Buddhist practice down at the foot of the altar. An adult, conscious of my actions, I was baptized the second time. This new birth took place in a Black church.

At Congdon Street Baptist Church and Immanuel Baptist Church, everyone took great joy in my accomplishments. I was a family member who had come from Cameroon via France. Never was I ostracized. I received nothing but love. For five years I was a member of Immanuel Baptist Church's board of trustees. Sincere and faithful friendships were born from my encounters with people who could have been my brothers, sisters, parents, or grandparents. They invited me for Thanksgiving, Christmas, and Easter meals. In the difficult moments that punctuate life, the Immanuel community was always there.

I will never forget the conversations I had with members of this surrogate family who told me about their childhood in the South of the United States. A close friend, who has died since, spoke about her grandmother who had been a slave. Her parents had worked miracles with next to nothing. I often went to visit her to hear about her memories of a simple but ever-so-heroic life. She described the bygone days of her childhood when people grew and bred everything that ended up on their plate. After World War II, her husband's regiment was stationed in Paris. The former soldier still had a few vestiges of the French he had picked up at the time. A young Parisian had taught him the rudiments of the language in exchange for a few cans of sardines. This man and his wife died three years apart. When she found herself alone after sixty-five years of marriage, the love of her children and grandchildren brought solace to her heart. This lady, who left us at the age of ninety-two, always had a smile on her face, no bitterness in her words, and infinite gratitude for the life God had granted her. Never did she vent about racism in America.

A friend I met at Immanuel Baptist Church hated movies about the lives of Black people during slavery and segregation. She preferred comedies by Tyler Perry or comforting and inspirational films. To her, Black suffering projected on the big screen was neither fictional nor entertaining. It was lodged in the depths of her being.

On my way to Sunday school, I would look forward to a hug from a lady who is, at the time of writing these lines, 103. Her distinctive elegance was ever present. Dressed in an off-white suit and a burgundy hat, her fingers adorned with jewels, she had a stately bearing and a reassuring expression on her face. Although she had lost her only son, this centenarian always had something encouraging and kind to say and a joy in sharing.

The Sunday-school teachers often recounted personal anecdotes to illustrate the day's lesson. They painted a picture of life as difficult, to be sure, but full of love and hope. Most of them had been activists in the 1960s and '70s. Their political commitments were inseparable from religious practice. Peace, love, and sharing were meaningless values if they did not lead to liberating human beings from the falseness of their lives. God's will is done on earth as it is in heaven. I was discovering a spiritual and political poetics that transformed my outlook on life.

The traditional Black church differs from megachurches, those huge evangelical churches that bring together more than 2,000 people and promote the gospel of prosperity. Unlike the latter, it participates in a long history of struggle for social justice. The slave revolt planned by Denmark Vesey (1822) and the one led by Pastor Nat Turner (1831) were of divine inspiration. Following in the footsteps of his father, Martin Luther King Jr. answered God's call and became a Baptist minister. His Christian beliefs and his commitment to Gandhi's philosophy of non-violence shaped his understanding of humanity and his struggle against racism, poverty, and militarism. The church is a pillar of the community. The dominical message is rooted in the political, economic, historical, and cultural reality of African Americans. Belief in the afterlife is not an expression of escapism. Jesus is a revolutionary. The point therefore is to transform the world we live in. It is in this way that churches are involved in community life. Christian groups set up food banks for the poor, tutor and mentor, provide economic assistance to families, serve hot meals in winter, educate parishioners on health issues, engage in real-estate investment to ensure affordable housing, hold discussions with politicians, and organize demonstrations against social injustice.

I moved to New York not long ago. On Sunday mornings I go to the famous Abyssinian Baptist Church in Harlem. I listen to a sermon that frees the captives. Born in blood, sweat, and tears, the songs say that nothing separates the believer from God's love. By praying, crying, and rejoicing in a community, a relationship is created between human beings that transcends particular interests. There is no attempt at proselytism in what I'm saying, only the need to explain the nature of my relationship with a part of the African American community.

When we non-native Blacks work hard, we are reaping the fruits from the grains of mustard seed that men and women deprived of freedom sowed in a hostile land. At the risk of offending some, it must be said loud and clear that we are not without responsibility. In public and in private, a greater number of us need to contribute to changing the racial dynamics. We need to get to know each other. As long as we accept the status quo, conflicts between African Americans and people of Caribbean or sub-Saharan origin will intrude in all areas of social life.

BLACK SCREEN: BRITS VERSUS ADOS

People of Afro-Caribbean and sub-Saharan African descent are blending willy-nilly into the African American community. Depending on their interests, they adopt an outward show of Black identity that gives them access to professional opportunities while allowing for a certain recognition within the power structure. In recent years, the presence of Black immigrants has become particularly pronounced in the film industry. *12 Years a Slave* (2013), *Selma* (2014), *Get Out* (2017), *Detroit* (2017), *Harriet* (2019), *Queen and Slim* (2019), and *Judas and the Black Messiah* (2021) are all films about the many facets African American lives. The main roles were given to actors who do not descend from this lineage: Chiwetel Ejiofor, Lupita Nyong'o, David Oyelowo, Carmen Ejogo, Daniel Kaluuya, John Boyega, and Cynthia Erivo. We might add Idris Elba to this list. Before he became known to the general public, Elba had gained a considerable reputation from his various parts in low-budget African American films, not to mention his role in the HBO series *The Wire*. With the exception of the Oscar-winner Nyong'o, who is Kenyan, all of the above actors are British citizens with Nigerian parents for the most part.[64]

All that viewers see onscreen are Black people. The phenotypical homogeneity conceals differences of identity and history. Lately this problem that seemed to oppose African Americans to Black Brits has been surfacing between sub-Saharan Africans. The Kenyan Nyong'o is producing the upcoming miniseries *Americanah*, based on Chimamanda Ngozi Adichie's best-selling novel about Nigerian immigration, identity, and race. She will also be playing the role of the main character, Ifemelu. As soon as the news was announced, Kenyans and Nigerians began to lay into each other on social networks, with some stubbornly insisting that the role should be played by a Nigerian actor, preferably an Igbo. Others argued that Nyong'o is one of the most widely recognized Black actors today and that the Oscar she received gives her unquestionable legitimacy.

The conflict between Black Brits and ADOS precedes the quarrel between Nigerians and Kenyans. Tariq Nasheed, Yvette Carnell, Antonio Moore, and other Black Media voices were the first to question the ways in which the African American experience is represented. Why doesn't Hollywood choose ADOS actors to play in films that tell their stories?

There are those who will point out that African Americans have on several occasions embodied African figures. Morgan Freeman played the role of Nelson Mandela in *Invictus* (2009); Forest Whitaker, the role of Idi Amin in *The Last King of Scotland* (2006);

---

64 Idris Elba's parents are from Sierra Leone and Ghana. Daniel Kaluuya was born in London to Ugandan parents.

Denzel Washington, that of Steve Biko in *Cry Freedom* (1987). I do not recall any opposition to the way Hollywood and African Americans appropriated these sub-Saharan stories. We might add to this list films such as *Coming to America* (1988), *Goodbye Bafana* (2007), *Endgame* (2009), and *Winnie Mandela* (2013).

Black Panther (2018), although it presented a fantasized image of a powerful Africa with a higher sense of morality than the West and depicted a kingdom where the subjects agree to submit to a benevolent king, was nonetheless quite well received on the continent and in the diaspora. It let the audience forget their degraded self-image for two hours and fifteen minutes. The beautiful, intelligent, and heroic characters provided Black viewers with a moment of enjoyment, at once collective and fleeting. It was like a relief valve for the excessive frustration with a reality that is stubborn and hard to change. One of my sisters reproached me for my critical take of the film. Her daughter had seen it twice on the big screen. No doubt it had a positive effect on the construction of my niece's imagination now that she was living in England. After a peaceful life in Cameroon, she had been discovering racism, day in and day out, from the mouths of the children in her private French school.

To return to African stories played by African American actors, there is good reason to contend that they perpetuate caricatures and stereotypes of sub-Saharan Africa. This I would not deny. It is not a matter of tit for tat. Many also maintain that an actor's greatness is measured by her ability to play any role, regardless of whether it has anything to do with who she is. Spike Lee and Ava DuVernay assert that Black Brits have superior classical training. Asked about the film *Get Out*, Samuel L. Jackson wondered whether the movie would have been more hard-hitting if the main character had been played by an African American. He thought that African American actors may have the existential baggage needed to give greater authenticity to the performance. He went on to imply that foreign actors were less expensive.

My focus here is not on the reasoning of advocates or adversaries of Black Brits, but on the political and economic dimension inherent in the presence of Blacks in Hollywood, a movie market originally intended for white audiences. It is for this very reason that an independent, community-based cinema has developed since the 1970s outside the major studios. The historic marginalization of Blacks and a shrinking imagination weigh on artistic production and performance. For many years, Hollywood films consigned African American actors to stock characters, such as the "magical negro" whose primary mission is to save the white hero. Some great names have played this role: Hattie McDaniel in *Gone with the Wind* (1939), Sidney Poitier in *The Defiant Ones* (1958) and *Guess Who's Coming to Dinner* (1967), Morgan Freeman in *Driving Ms. Daisy* (1989) and *Bruce Almighty* (2003), Whoopi Goldberg in *Ghost* (1990), Denzel Washington in *Philadelphia* (1993), Will Smith in *The Legend of Bagger Vance* (2000), and Viola Davis in *The Help* (2011).

The magical negro can be a faithful slave who helps raise a white girl, a doctor in love with a young white woman, the chauffeur of an elderly white woman, a medium who puts two lovers separated by death in contact with each other, a lawyer defending a person with AIDS who has suffered discrimination, the providential caddy of a golfer, or a housekeeper who develops a deep affective bond with a white child. The mission of the magical negro is always the same: to contribute to the fulfillment of the white person. Consequently, the character, whether or not it is a stereotype, remains trapped in the role of a helper. And regardless of social status and historical condition, this well-meaning, debonair figure defuses conflicts. The magical negro supports the white protagonist in the accomplishment of the latter's destiny and brings out their unsuspected human qualities.[65]

In *Monster's Ball* (2001), Leticia Musgrove (Halle Berry) has a memorable sexual relationship with Hank Grotowski (Billy Bob Thornton). Hank comes from a racist family that has worked on death row for three generations—father, son, and grandson. Leticia does not know that Hank participated in the execution of her husband Lawrence Musgrove (Sean Combs). When Leticia's son is hit by a car, Hank drives them to the hospital where the child dies. This strange unexpected encounter creates an undying bond between the two characters. When she is evicted from her home, Hank decides to provide for the lonely and destitute black woman. By the magic of intimacy, the mere presence of Leticia in Hank's life allows him to expiate his racist attitude.

The magical negro crosses different periods. The character plays a redemptive role in a country where the political situation and the Hollywood psyche are often two sides of the same coin. I am thinking here of the famous *Birth of a Nation* (1915), whose racist imagination reinforced the oppressive practices of white supremacists in the United States. The Black man is depicted as a savage

---

65 Kwame Anthony Appiah, "No Bad Nigger: Blacks as the Ethical Principle in the Movies" in Marjorie Garber, Jann Malock, and Rebecca L. Walkowitz (eds), *Media Spectacles* (New York: Routledge, 1993), pp. 77–90.

beast from which white women must be protected, in essence a rapist who deserves the lynching he gets.

Hollywood today has decided to stray off the beaten path and explore hitherto occulted historical figures and stories of life. It is only fitting that African Americans not be kept out of these new representations. The fight for citizenship is not limited to civil rights; it also takes place on the big screen. Given the long-term struggle led by ADOS actors, the over-representation of Black Brits in highly symbolic films now provokes movements of protest.

Cynthia Erivo was chosen to play the role of the abolitionist Harriet Tubman, one of the icons of African American freedom. When the news was announced in September 2018, ADOS immediately expressed disgruntlement, but it fell on deaf ears. A year later, the dormant anger was reignited with the release of the movie trailer and the appearance of Erivo's tweets mocking the "ghetto accent" of African Americans. A call went out to boycott the film: #boycottharriet, #HarrietDeservesBetter. Carnell and Moore demanded that the actor confirm or deny reports that she was from an Igbo lineage that was involved in human trafficking during the slave trade. To dismiss out of hand this outpouring of frustration would be dishonest.

White actors can be violent, cruel, criminal, and immoral without reflecting on every other individual whose phenotype they share. Relieved of the burden of race, they can embody a humanity free from stereotypes and from the unrealistic expectations of a population thirsting to see itself on the screen. Black actors, on the other hand, are well aware that race is more a factor of exclusion than inclusion. When a Black director or actor receives an Oscar, the event is historical and collective. The victory is not individual.

Its symbolic power extends beyond the borders of the United States. The achievement belongs by proxy to all people of sub-Saharan origin. It is proof through images that, if Hollywood—i.e. the whites—gave them the opportunity, Black people could, sporadically, become part of the great family of cinema.

Black Brits admit that they are now looking to Hollywood for work. If the film industry in Great Britain were more open and concerned about including the country's Black populations in the cinematographic imagination, these actors would probably not be as present in the American movie scene. In 2016, Will Smith, Jada Pinket, and Spike Lee initiated #OscarsSoWhite, denouncing the lack of diversity. Three years later, are we witnessing the birth of #HollywoodSoBlackBrits? The opposition between Black British and American actors is only one of the many manifestations of the struggle for economic and artistic survival in a white-supremacist world.

As we can see from the sharp criticism of Barack Obama, Kamala Harris, and Black Brits, the power of symbols has become fallible. Black faces from other places have lost their hypnotic inspirational power. They have become the visible embodiment of the figure of the usurper that extends now to all immigrants or descendants of Afro-Caribbean and Sub-Saharan immigrants. ADOS vehemently assert that we do not care about the African American condition. We prosper at their expense, reaping the benefits of a political struggle we did not wage and of a suffering we never experienced. We are seizing opportunities meant for them. The grievances are not confined to the competition for limited positions. Taken to the extreme, this logic turns the Black immigrant or descendant of immigrants into an objective ally of white supremacy, contributing to the oppression of ADOS in an active or passive way.

According to Carnell and Moore's ideological outlook, all sub-Saharans are descendants of people who sold captives to the whites, unless they can prove their innocence. The distinction between ADOS and Blacks of immigrant origin is established by turning genealogy into an unstoppable weapon of discrimination. The very presence of Afro-Caribbean and sub-Saharans in certain spheres of political power, the media or academia is seen as a form of injustice provoking a combination of bitterness and animosity. Why them and not us? Whether we are ADOS, Blacks from sub-Saharan Africa or from the Caribbean, identity conflicts between the different groups raise questions of relationship, responsibility, respect, and loyalty.

The Black Baptist Church in America has unquestionably structured my relationship with African Americans. Right or wrong, I have the firm conviction that I need to give back to the community of the living and the dead what it has given me. I am never alone. A flock of witnesses who walked through fire without being reduced to ashes accompany me. They expand the breadth of possibilities; they trace with the ink of suffering the possibilities of hope. The road that led me to the Graduate Center at CUNY in New York City was paved with historical disasters that preceded my coming into the world. I am not self-made. It all began in Cameroon where I was given a quality education. In France, the college education I received at no cost taught me to reject fundamentalist identity discourses that dictate that reading works by white men is traumatizing. My teachers were often distant but passionate and conscientious.

I loved reading, studying, and writing about Victor Hugo's *Les Misérables*, Franz Kafka's *Metamorphosis*, La Bruyère's *Les Caractères*, Dostoevsky's *The Idiot*, or Goethe's *The Sorrows of Young Werther*. My love for philosophy began in the last year of high school when I was introduced to the subject for the first time, and it has only grown over the years. The flexibility of the American university system gave me the opportunity during my literature studies to read Jean-Paul Sartre, Karl Jaspers, Sören Kierkegaard, Simone Weil, Hannah Arendt, Emmanuel Levinas, Walter Benjamin, Michel Foucault, Jacques Derrida, Cioran, and so many others who have helped me to think about a whole range of issues. I sometimes tell my students that there is an invisible community of Europeans whom I consult regularly. Some are philosophers; others, musicians or painters.

Knowledge must be decolonized and school curricula diversified. But we must not reproduce what the West is accused of doing—that is, eradicating that intimate part of the self that we recognize in others and limiting the possibilities of the human being within the narrow confines of race understood as identity in essentialist terms. This is a categorical imperative in the Kantian sense of the term: "Act only on that maxim whereby thou canst at the same time will that it should become a universal law."[66]

Some years back, I imagined a diasporic consciousness that I termed *melancholia africana*,[67] which made it possible to examine

---

66 Immanuel Kant, *Groundwork of the Metaphysics of Morals* (1785) (Mary Gregor ed. and trans.; Kristin M. Korsgaard introd.) (Cambridge: Cambridge University Press, 1998), p. 178.

67 Nathalie Etoke, *Melancholia Africana: The Indispensable Overcoming of the Black Condition* (Bill Hamlett trans.) (London and New York: Rowman & Littlefield International, 2019).

loss, grief, and survival in continental and diasporic Africa. I felt
that skin color, the material and historical conditions of Black existence had overshadowed an interiority that needed to be exposed.
Developing an awareness of the self in relationship to the tensions
inherent in the emergence of freedom seemed fundamental to me.
The struggle starts with the self. The current debate on reparations
and the emergence of the ADOS movement testify to a community of destiny that is both frustrated and fragmented. The majority
of Black immigrants leave their countries of origin for economic
reasons. Statistically speaking, African Americans are at the bottom
of the social ladder. There are also pockets of poverty within the
Afro-Caribbean and sub-Saharan communities. However, the
problems raised by the ADOS movement stand in counterpoint
to the success of these two groups.

Social disparities and the myth of the American dream mod-
ulate a relationship to liberation founded on the model of capitalist
democracies: the right to private property and capital. Capitalist
democracies are inegalitarian regimes. They have created narratives
that justify inequality while claiming to put an end to it. The clash
between ADOS and Blacks of immigrant origin belongs to the
capitalist ideological continuum. They do not challenge it. Since
both parties wish only to profit from capitalism, I do not advocate
or suggest developing a strategy of solidarity that would contribute
in the end to strengthening a system underpinned by disparities.
The present-day conflict is one of the many consequences of a
political and economic doctrine that Thomas Piketty proposes to
overcome.[68] Indeed, we must find a way out of capitalism, not for
Black people but for the majority of human beings.

---

68 Thomas Piketty, *Capital and Ideology* (Arthur Goldhammer trans.) (Cambridge,
MA: Harvard University Press, 2019).

CAPITALISM, THE AMERICAN DREAM, AND LIBERATION

The failure of communism put an end to the prospect of a radical alternative to capitalism. With the exception of anarchists or members of the far left, we have all more or less accepted capitalism, democracy, and the American dream. We formulate analyses from an immutable paradigmatic starting point. As a result, criticism becomes a metalanguage that serves not so much to abolish the capitalism-democracy-American-dream triad as to promote redemptive narratives that make it seem accessible to all. The problem is considered the solution. We fail to consider that, from an epistemological standpoint, the possibilities of this triad are established on the basis of a conceptual framework that excludes and oppresses non-white populations. What authorizes us to believe that today it will make free individuals of us? We want to think that capitalism, democracy, and the American dream are perfectible or reformable. But what we are endorsing in reality is the idea of capitalism with a human face whose modus operandi would be a form of neoliberal social democracy that flirts with the welfare state without advocating socialism.

The radical transformation of a society requires establishing a collective imagination that begins by questioning and rejecting prefabricated paradigms that have been imposed by violence. As Western societies face a rise of populism, there is talk of a crisis of democracy and capitalism—two totems that have had disastrous consequences on the lives of entire populations from the very outset. What could capitalist democracy and human rights possibly mean to Native American victims of genocide, or sub-Saharans, first enslaved and then colonized? What do they signify to descendants of slaves? Nothing but tasteless jokes. Ideological

94

hogwash. Some will ask me: "What are you complaining about? The American capitalist democracy makes your life pleasant." But seen from the perspective of suffering humanity, what does the purported success of a handful of individuals represent? Is this the legacy, is this the future we are leaving to posterity? Be selfish. Worry about your own well-being. Wallow in nihilistic hedonism. Such a choice reflects our participation in a campaign of mass destruction that will leave no survivors.

During the 1970s, the struggle for Black liberation espoused a fundamentally anti-capitalist Marxist agenda. Stokely Carmichael asserted that the capitalist system is inseparable from racism, that it cannot create an economic structure free of exploitation.[69] Comparing capitalism to a sinking ship, George Jackson asked Black Americans why they were rushing to board it.[70] The words of these two revolutionaries find little resonance today. Black populations are hierarchized. Social success and home ownership will not liberate the majority.

The fact is, whether we are African, Afro-Caribbean, or African American, we all want a piece of the capitalist cake. Nothing new in this behavior. All human beings now share it. Capitalism is a steamroller and it is doomed to failure. The opposition between ADOS and Black non-descendants of American slavery proves that historically oppressed populations will never benefit from a socioeconomic system founded on inequalities. In theory, meritocracy is about advancement through skills and it

69 Stokely Carmichael, *Stokely Speaks: From Black Power to Pan-Africanism* (Chicago: Chicago Review Press, 2007), p. 87

70 George Jackson, *Soledad Brother: The Prison Letters of George Jackson* (Chicago: Lawrence Hill Books, 1994), p. 254.

should induce social mobility. But in point of fact, in a capitalist regime, it participates in the creation of an elite and the depoliti-cization[71] of the problem of inequality, thereupon seen as resulting from the inherent deficiency of those individuals that American society dubs losers.

Socioeconomic disparities, when depoliticized, are not regarded as embedded in a historical context that compels us to acknowledge the dynamics of power. Instead of transforming society, we are sum-moned to adapt to a system that organizes and justifies inequalities. Socioeconomic imbalances are perceived as objective realities that the subject should transcend. The ability to climb the ladder through talent and hard work is purported to guarantee all individuals a place in the dominant structure. And so the conversation is shifted from political struggles to the behavior and attitude of people. Whence the conclusion that Blacks of sub-Saharan and Afro-Caribbean immigrant origin are hard-working and disciplined, while African Americans, in addition to being lazy, feel that every-thing is coming to them. This type of narrative legitimizes inequal-ity and the downward mobility of a human group. The success of Black immigrants and the failure of ADOS testify to the intersec-tion of the depoliticization of inequalities and the normalization of social injustice.

Instead of examining the relationship between the American dream and racism, we question our ability to play a game whose rules were written in the tears, blood, and the cries of the indige-nous populations who are victims of genocide. We merrily wallow

---

71 I am drawing on Wendy Brown's work on depoliticization: *Regulating Aversion: Tolerance in the Age of Identity and Empire* (Princeton, NJ and Oxford: Princeton University Press, 2006).

in a white-supremacist amnesia where indigenous populations are ghostly, voiceless silhouettes that do not deprive us of sleep. The presence in the United States of a Black population from the Caribbean and sub-Saharan Africa is part and parcel of an imperialist continuum: the post-colonial state's failure, neo-colonialism, the import of labor, globalization, and the neoliberal model of success. The ADOS movement demands reparations. African Americans are entitled to recognition, as were the other groups that have received compensation for the United States' historic wrongs.

Blacks of immigrant origin benefit from affirmative action. The accomplishments of these Africans and Afro-Caribbeans do not culminate in a collective movement against racism. The successful members of these groups, who belong to Black elite, are mainly involved in community and charitable organizations focused on the development of their countries of origin or the situation of their nationals on American soil. Since the priorities of Blacks from elsewhere are different from those of indigenous Blacks, the ADOS movement wants to reorganize the system of preferential selection to cater primarily to descendants of slaves born in the United States.

In addition to reparations, Black Media activists have put forward specific policy measures that take into account the social and economic situation of African Americans: priority in access to housing, credit, and free health care, public education reform, etc. I do not question the legitimacy of these demands, but there is a problematical aspect to the ADOS ideology—namely, a form of ethno-genealogical chauvinism coupled with a nativist discourse[72]

---

72 Nativism is a political current born in countries of immigrants such as the United States, Canada, or Australia. Descendants of immigrants assert an

that espouses the contours of American imperialism and exceptionalism. Indeed, when the ideologues talk of lineage, they are
actually referring to the "right of blood" and the privileges that are
supposed to follow from it. Political identity is connected to a narrative in which genealogy and oppression justify selection, distinction, and hierarchization based on DNA.

Historically speaking, the result of this type of classification
and reasoning has been catastrophic for humanity. Giving ADOS
preference or priority is associated with the idea of a superiority
that derives legitimacy from the status of victim. It is a matter of
exercising one's political and social power from a position of inferiority due to the legacy of slavery and racism that the American
nation must take into account in its relationship with African
Americans. My intention is not, of course, to ascribe genocidal
intentions to the ADOS movement. Black Media leaders have
never called for the extermination or exploitation of people from
sub-Saharan Africa or the Caribbean. The genealogical and pro-
capitalist approach simply demonstrates ideological regression and
the heightened tension of the political imaginary.

The ADOS movement evidences the existence of an African
American population that scorns the pan-African dream born in
the heart of uprooted Afro-descendant populations searching for
an original matrix. It amplifies the end of solidarity politics, the
abandonment of anti-imperialist and anti-capitalist struggles.
Some believe that these struggles trap African Americans in a

---

exclusive right of ownership over the territory and claim benefits related to their
status. They oppose the presence of newcomers. The nativists are of European origin and promote white supremacy. In adopting this nativist discourse, ADOS
position themselves in a logic whose origins are racist.

foreignness that keeps them from identifying with their country, and thereby legitimate the exclusion and devalorization from which they suffer. Claiming membership in the American nation now seems to be incompatible with a convergence of fights for the freedom of all.

Martin Luther King Jr. believed that the struggle for national liberation in Africa served as a catalyst for African Americans to achieve full civil rights.[73] And when Malcolm X created the Organization of African-American Unity, he declared: "We [. . .] join hands and hearts with all the people of African origin in a grand alliance by forgetting all the differences that the power structure has created to keep us divided and enslaved. We further pledge to strengthen our common goal: freedom from oppression."[74]

Destroying the tyrannical structures and institutions responsible for the established order is no longer of relevance. Rather, the focus is on occupying a privileged position in an inegalitarian system. The ADOS movement hopes that reforming this system will make it more just. As a precondition, populations deemed foreign and usurping are to be excluded. Carnell and Moore demand reparations but do not reject the capitalist ideology behind the transatlantic slave trade. They do not call into question private property, wealth accumulation, or the market economy. What they want is to have access to them. They rail against an America that has sidelined them and call on the American government to set up mechanisms to redistribute wealth acquired by the sweat of their ancestors' brow.

---

73 Martin Luther King Jr., *Why We Can't Wait* (Boston, MA: Beacon Press, 2010), p. 15.

74 Malcolm X, *February 1965: The Final Speeches* (New York: Pathfinder, 1992), p. 291.

Such an initiative would make the mass participation of ADOS in the capitalist system possible.

Whether we are ADOS, Afro-Caribbean, or Africans, our existential paths have been traced inside the matrix of white power. The opposition today between the different components of the Black community reveals tensions and fault lines. Race and the identification of a common enemy do not create bonds anymore. The idea of a common destiny, which seemed so strong in the 1970s, is more fragile than ever, and even inexistent in some circles of thought. We never really examined the nature of a bond that contained the seeds of its own destruction. Wherever we are, regardless of the cultural, political, and identity specificities of each group, as long as we do not establish strategies of anti-imperialist and anti-capitalist resistance, a few of us will continue to be part of the white power structure while the majority will be left out. Whether in sub-Saharan Africa, the Caribbean, or the United States, the existence of a Black bourgeoisie has never helped the lumpenproletariat.

Prisoners of their economic situation in the diaspora or on the continent, people of African descent are neo-slaves: "If you don't make any more wages than you need to live, you are a neoslave. [. . .] Neoslavery is an economic condition [. . .] which manifests itself in the total loss or absence of self-determination."[75] In addition to economic devalorization, Black bodies are also victims of violence perpetrated by brutal democratic or post-colonial policing. Uprisings are called riots and repressed by the police state, which does not defend the interests of workers or outcasts. Whether we are African, Afro-Caribbean, or African American, we share the

75 Jackson, *Soledad Brother*, p. 252.

same existential insecurity. Because we strive to apply, copy, or fit into patterns imposed by imperialist democracies, no matter where we are, our collective inability to determine or control our conditions of living is a millstone that we carry assiduously around our necks.

Mainstream thinking would like us to believe that, without capitalism and Westernization, the door to the future would be locked: "all languages, religions, ways of thinking and living [left] forever in the past of modernity!"[76] I am not advocating a return to the lost origins of some mythical Africa that none of my contemporaries ever experienced. Rather, it is a matter of seeing how the world of the past remains present in our daily lives, of choosing what will enable us to move forward, and getting rid of everything that keeps us in a passive situation once and for all.

Given the damage European domination caused, we can only conclude that pre-colonial Africa was undoubtedly riven by inner frailties and permeable to external influences. The internal devastation goes hand in hand with a mimetic obsession that is doomed to failure. We must "establish new practices and conceptions of politics and economics, ethics and philosophy, technology and social organization that will be motivated by people's well-being rather than progress or economic growth."[77]

Before definitively leaving his native land, the sociologist W. E. B. Du Bois explained the reasons for this departure in a letter to a friend. Disillusioned by the situation of African Americans,

---

76 Walter D. Mignolo, *La désobéissance épistémique: Rhétorique de la modernité, logique de la colonialité et grammaire de la décolonialité* (Brussels: P.I.E Peter Lang, 2015), p. 57.

77 Mignolo, *La désobéissance épistémique*, p. 57.

he confided to her that they were not in a position to win the fight against racism and capitalism. So he and his wife sold their house and bought a one-way ticket to Accra.[78] Du Bois bitterly recognized that the American democracy was a dead end for the descendants of slaves. The dice were loaded from the very start. Unlike Marcus Garvey, who advocated separatism and a return of Blacks from the diaspora to Africa to assume power there, Du Bois devoted his life to fighting for the integration of Blacks into American society. In parallel to this struggle, he was an ardent supporter of independence in Africa. At age 93, he left his homeland permanently, renounced his US citizenship, and became an official member of the Communist Party.

Du Bois answered Kwame Nkrumah's appeal for help in developing a strategy for the global liberation of the continent. At that time, a handful of African American artists, athletes, intellectuals, and revolutionaries were living in Africa or had spent time there. The struggle against oppression in Africa and in the diaspora gave the project of returning to the continent a singular thrust: to imagine together and then bring into being a world where Blacks from everywhere would be free.

As small as they may be, communities of African Americans exist that have chosen to live in Africa, particularly in Ghana. They did not wait for Ghanaian president Nana Akufo-Addo to proclaim 2019 the Year of Return. Tourism to places of memory has become a big business. It is called slavery (heritage) tourism. The Year of Return coincided with the celebration of 400 years since the arrival of the first enslaved Africans in Jamestown, Virginia.

---

78 W. E. B Du Bois, Letter to Grace Goens, September 13, 1961. Available at: https://bit.ly/3hr8M6Q (last accessed on August 25, 2020).

Coming back home was reserved for the privileged. A relationship was established between the Ghanaian state and the diaspora in which memory, desire, and affect became the object of a transaction. President Akufo-Addo targeted celebrities and a category of African Americans with above-average financial means. It was specifically stated that participating parties "accept to see social relations recreated to meet the needs of the 'expansive dynamics'." With each tourist spending an average of 1,850 dollars, the Ghanaian Ministry of Tourism expected to earn 925 million dollars in dividends, 50 percent more than in 2018.[79]

Ghana maintains and promotes places of memory to fill government coffers. People living in tourist areas sell souvenirs to visitors. The capitalist logic is constantly reinventing itself. The descendants of those who were sold now represent a gold mine.[80] They are Americans of sub-Saharan origin. Their African side opens up the field of capitalist possibilities that situate human relations in terms of interest and profit. No doubt, the Ghanaian government does not imagine using a portion of the profits, however tiny, to renew the connection between Africa and the diaspora by supporting non-profit organizations or initiatives in Harlem, Baltimore, or south Chicago.

---

79 Stéphane Haber, "Le néolibéralisme est-il une phase du capitalisme?" *Raisons politiques* 52 (2013); 25–35; here, p. 26.

80 Gina Paige, co-founder of the genetic testing company African Ancestry, says "there's a direct correlation to the release of the movie *Black Panther*" and "a tripling of visits to AfricanAncestry.com". Quoted in Clara Germani, "On US Slavery's 400th Anniversary, How Ancestry Quests Help Heal," *Christian Science Monitor*, August 26, 2019. Available at: https://bit.ly/2Je7Oin (last accessed on November 25, 2020).

Capitalist thinking is inseparable from imperialism and racism. It will not save us. When people of sub-Saharan origin adopt this way of thinking, the result is cognitive dissonance and ideological incongruities which lead to conflicts such as the one currently opposing ADOS to Blacks of immigrant origin. Liberation strategies have been buried in the garish grave of capitalist democracy. Extricating oneself from the category of working poor to join the middle class has become the *sine qua non* of liberation. Regardless of political affiliations, it is the self-same ideology of promoting a bourgeois citizenship that would guarantee disadvantaged populations the possibility of belonging to a social group with access to property and capital. Notwithstanding the individual success stories we are fed, when it comes to minorities, capitalist democracy excludes more than it includes. This model of society highlights singularities or a group of people who are not representative of the marginalized community. The exceptional nature of a minority's success does not protect it from racism. Nor does it bring significant benefits to the oppressed majority. Whether on the continent or in the diaspora, the appropriation of the oppressor's weapons leads to collective suicide. Let us not forget Audre Lorde's prophetic words: "For the master's tools will never dismantle the master's house. They may allow us temporarily to beat him at his own game, but they will never enable us to bring about genuine change."[81]

Standing at the impassable wall of our failures, it becomes incumbent upon us to create a radical and transformative political imagination that will save humankind from its programmed

---

81 Audre Lorde, "The Master's Tools Will Never Dismantle the Master's House" in *Sister Outsider. Essays and Speeches* (Berkeley, CA: Crossing Press, 1984), p. 112.

annihilation. We live in a society where everything is expected to be accomplished effortlessly and very quickly, including finding a formula to solve a centuries-old problem. Radical change requires both collective and critical reflection. Capitalism is running out of steam. Poor white populations blame foreigners for their woes. Yet it is not the foreigner who decides to lower the cost of labor, to relocate companies, or to open borders. Blacks of immigrant origin have now become the scapegoats of ADOS. Some Africans and Afro-Caribbeans prosper in an inegalitarian society with no concern for the history that makes their upward mobility possible. We need to challenge the capitalist dogma that shapes the way we look at the world, and then devise forms of direct democracy that are in touch with the complexity of our economic, political, and cultural situation.

As long as we continue to claim the symbols of our oppression as our own, in the name of our individual freedom, we will never be collectively free.

CHAPTER 3

Decolonizing Freedom

The report stated that public officials of the judicial system of Los Angeles routinely used the acronym N.H.I to refer to any case involving a breach of rights of young Black males who belong to the jobless category of the inner city ghettoes. N.H.I means "no humans involved."

Sylvia Wynter[1]

"Unarmed Black Man Killed by Police" is a frequent front-page headline. If Black police officers are involved in cases of police brutality, the conservative media love to call attention to the fact in an attempt to deracialize the clash and eradicate the causal relationship between institutional racism and oppression. After all, if the police officer is Black, then the incident cannot be racially motivated. But in the pervading culture of professions such as policing, the Black man is irrevocably categorized as a potential criminal or a repeat offender. The fact that some Black police officers are more

---

1 Sylvia Wynter, "No Humans Involved: An Open Letter to My Colleagues," *Forum N.H.I Knowledge for the 21st Century* 1(1) (Fall 1994): 42–73; here, p. 42.

violent toward individuals whose phenotype they share should come as no surprise. Racism is not just about color. Police officers, regardless of their skin color, are the armed instrument of the state. Being black-skinned does not mean that one necessarily shares a world view, an emotional bond, or a sense of loyalty with all black-skinned people. Slaves on the plantations were sometimes guarded by other slaves, carefully chosen by the plantation owner. Already at that time, some Blacks killed others on behalf of the Master. The whites who bought captives on the African coasts had accomplices on the continent, who organized the capture of free men, women, and children in order to deliver them to the whites. Although these intermediaries never defined themselves as Black because it was not part of the conception they had of their identity, the fact that Blacks sold other Blacks is hammered home again and again. Individuals who collaborate with the oppressive structure have always existed and are not likely to disappear anytime soon. To hold them up in an attempt to rationalize the irrational or justify the unjustifiable is a rhetorical sleight of hand that deceives only those who are susceptible to this kind of manipulation.

The video of Walter Scott's killing on April 4, 2015 in North Charleston, South Carolina, reminded me of two essential truths: the historical devalorization of the lives of Black people and the ongoing denial of their humanity. As I watched Scott fleeing Michael T. Slager, I thought of the slaves trying to escape without knowing where they were going. Although gripped by fear, they found courage in their legs and hope in their hearts. Any white man could carry them back to the plantation, take possession of their life, or kill them. Yet they kept running, toward freedom . . . Running in an open-air prison. Comparing the fatal destiny of the escaped-then-captured slave to that of Scott might seem anachronistic and hyperbolic. Nevertheless, the will to escape the oppressor lives on.

These incidents are recurrent in the underprivileged neighborhoods of twenty-first-century America. When Black women, men, teenagers, and children confront the police, they are often facing death. Scott, a Black man over fifty—a son, a brother, a father—was stopped for a non-functioning brake light. He ran from Slager who had fired his Taser in an attempt to overpower him. Scott ran, ran, and ran. Slager, a white officer behind him, gunned down a nigger. Unable to catch Scott, Slager fired eight shots in a row at Scott's back as Scott collapsed to the ground.

The video shows a public execution. His exploit accomplished, Slager called his superiors, and asserted without blinking an eye that Scott had tried to take his Taser from him. The police officer went to the trouble of placing the Taser next to his victim's lifeless body. Prior to the release of the video, the official version only mentioned the legitimacy of the officer's fear for his life.

As horrifying as it was, what happened to Walter Scott was predictable. What happened to Walter Scott had happened to others. What happened to Walter Scott will happen again. The Black victim of white violence is a historical commonplace. Heir to a long tradition, Michael T. Slager was perpetuating the foundational violence. Despite the ideological propaganda—the Doctrine of Discovery[2] and the allegory of Manifest Destiny—everyone

---

2 In 1452 Pope Nicholas V issued the papal bull Dum Diversas, granting the king of Portugal "full and free permission to invade, search out, capture, and subjugate the Saracens and pagans and any other unbelievers and enemies of Christ wherever they may be, as well as their kingdoms, duchies, counties, principalities, and

knows that America, as a nation and economic power, was born from the extermination of the Native Americans followed by the enslavement of the sub-Saharans.

Appearances notwithstanding, non-white populations are not the only victims of the violence inherent in the process of domination. The conqueror is also an oppressor who must ask himself about his own humanity. What happens in his soul and conscience when he opts to normalize the dehumanization of non-white people, to appropriate land and humans pronounced savages? When the police institution is called upon to assume responsibility for the deeds of its members, it defends itself saying that there are only a few black sheep, that not all police officers are racist, and that there was no intention to kill. The institution cannot be separated from society, neither can men from their deeds. A human group has been historically constructed as non-human and the other as the accomplished form of absolute and superior humanity across time and space.

Blacks were sold, raped, and lynched. America's oppressive practices toward the Black population shape the ways in which

---

other property [. . .] and to reduce their persons into perpetual slavery" (Cited in Diana Hayes, "Reflections on Slavery" in Charles E. Curran [ed.], *Change in Official Catholic Moral Teachings* [New York: Paulist Press], pp. 65–75; here, p. 67). Three years later, Nicholas V issued a second bull, Romanux Pontifex, that confirmed the first.

The application of this text was extended to every Christian/European nation. The right to take possession of land, without any regard to the people who resided there, was conceptualized around the idea of discovery. I learned in primary school that Christopher Columbus discovered America. I also remember all the agents of European domination whose names we had to memorize: Vasco da Gama, Ferdinand Magellan, Bartholomeu Diaz, Mungo Park. The history books called them explorers.

police violence and contemporary racial injustice are understood and represented. The past is a prologue. During the period of slavery, being human meant being white and free. Every white person embodied a certain level of power. Legal or illegal, the use of violence—both physical and psychological—has been the most effective instrument for controlling, disciplining, and subjugating the Black population. The founding fathers are referred to in glorifying terms devoid of criticism. The creative genius of the conquering and civilizing white male ego conceptualized and enacted the project of slave dehumanization and imperialist expansion. White American masculinity derives its coherence from the oppression of the Native American and sub-Saharan populations. To be free in the American slave state is to not be Black. To be free is to not be in chains. To be free is to be able to exercise an economic, political, cultural, and ontological domination over Blacks.

If we look at the origins of the police and the judiciary in this country, clearly the primary intention never was to protect Black people. The point was to terrorize them in order to consign them to spaces of non-being. The police enforced a racist social order. The legal system was biased. The complicity of the two institutions was directed toward subjecting Black people to a miserable existence, thus forcing them to accept their sub-human status. Let us not forget the slavery, the segregation, and the Jim Crow laws. Let us not forget the lynchings, the collective merriment of white men and women with their little blond-haired children gathering around a tree. Their eyes glowing with morbid enjoyment, they would revel at the sight of the "strange fruit."[3]

---

3 Song made famous by Billie Holiday, the lyrics of which were written by Abel Meeropol, an American Jewish songwriter, better known under his pseudonym Lewis Allan.

Let us not forget the Ku Klux Klan. Let us not forget Emmett Till. Where were the police? What did the courts do? To reinforce and protect white power—that is to say, the freedom of whites—such is the original mission of the police in America. Since the abolition of slavery, the two institutions—the police and the judiciary—have continued to work well together. Police brutality, mass incarceration, and social inequality are the exorbitant price that Black people pay for white freedom. When white police officers kill Black women, children, and men, they are brutalizing not human beings but the descendants of slaves, whose skin manifests their sub-humanity. In the United States of America, to call oneself Black and human is an existential oxymoron. In the white gaze, the Black population embodies "an absence of human presence."[4] As a result, the refusal to see oneself in the Other has sedimented over the centuries into an inability to establish a human connection with the dehumanized.

It is in this context that whites appear as "moral monsters."[5] Held to be self-evident moral principles, reciprocity, respect, human dignity, and good and evil actually vary according to circumstances, when they do not simply disappear in the relationship that is maintained with Black people. The result is an inversion of the moral order, with the creation of an ethics of self-protection in which evil is no longer negative because the fear of the Other who is not us justifies violence. Darren Wilson, the white police officer who

---

4 Lewis R. Gordon, *Existentia Africana: Understanding Africana Existential Thought* (New York and London: Routledge, 2000), p. 61.

5 I borrow this expression from James Baldwin. See *Conversations with James Baldwin* (Fred L. Stanley and Louis H. Pratt eds) (Jackson: University Press of Mississippi, 1989), p. 41.

murdered Michael Brown in Fergusson, Missouri, on August 9, 2014, declared that Brown had the most intense aggressive face he had ever seen. The angry young man looked to him like a grunting demon. Wilson's vocabulary describes at best a wild beast that must be urgently overcome, at worst a supernatural and diabolical creature.

The abolition of slavery and the end of segregation did not liberate the American conscience from its moral monsters. The white mental reservoir is cluttered with images, at once frozen and fictitious, of Blacks who are neither brothers nor sisters nor children with whom one could identify. When Black individuals are not seen in terms of this stunted imaginary, they are maintained in a state of permanent infantilization. The Other knows better the origin and the solution to their problems and refuses to see them as individuals capable of autonomy. Whence the desire to help or rescue these creatures burdened with a deficit of humanity. As long as the foul beast dwelling within certain white minds is not unmasked, no laws will protect Black people. No justice will ever truly be achieved.

The media plays a key role in the degradation of Black lives. News camera crews were mobilized to cover the riots in the wake of Freddie Gray's suspicious death in Baltimore in April 2015. Bill O'Reilly exploded in a string of racist stereotypes to which viewers of his Fox News show *The O'Reilly Factor* are accustomed.[6] Black Americans were criminals, he said, and therefore deserved to be

---

6 Fox News fired the star TV host in April 2017 after it emerged that he had settled a series of sexual harassment lawsuits out of court. Before being toppled by the Me Too movement, the immense renown that O'Reilly enjoyed went unabated.

imprisoned. Not only did they have tattoos on their faces but they also could barely read or write, which was why they could not get jobs.[7] The generalizing statements were aired on a conservative station that is in the habit of attacking Blacks and Latinx. In the American historical context, these stereotypes and prejudices about Black people not only reinforce old representations but also solidify their present-day relevance by lodging them in a permanent power relationship.

To clear police officers of responsibility for crimes, O'Reilly also brandishes high statistics of "Black-on-Black crime." The commentator's argumentative arsenal is aimed at delegitimizing the urban revolt. His discourse justifies the use of violence on a crowd of undisciplined "rioters" who do not respect the law. A video of a Black mother reprimanding her son whom she had recognized as one of the young men throwing stones at the police was broadcast by the media ad nauseam. Overnight Toya Graham was brought out of the shadows into the limelight before lapsing once again into oblivion. Promises of work were dangled before her eyes on TV. Oprah Winfrey presented her with a 15,000-dollar check. An anonymous donor paid her rent for a few months. A fundraising platform raised 12,000 dollars for her. The woman owed her fleeting notoriety to the combination of slaps and furious words that she meted out to her son. Her greatest fear was that her offspring would meet Freddie Gray's fate. Graham was invited to appear on TV shows. She was even awarded the title of Mother of the Year by some. Others made of her a hero. Progressives were outraged.

---

7 *Bill O'Reilly's Talking Points*, "The Baltimore Rioting Now Leading to Madness," Fox News, April 30, 2015. Available at: https://bit.ly/3llGJYM (last accessed on August 26, 2020).

Conservatives applauded. Watching this appalling spectacle on my TV screen left me speechless.

By focusing on the vandalism and on Toya Graham's behavior, media coverage of the uprisings in Ferguson and then in Baltimore diverted attention from police brutality. Scenes of chaos in the streets were described as resulting from illegitimate acts of violence. Moralistic rhetoric about the destruction of property evacuated the issue of racism. Burned or looted stores triggered outbursts of righteous indignation. But the death of innocent people at the hands of the police did not make right-thinking America's blood curdle. Instead, people were outraged by the destruction of a drugstore. Businesses had to be protected. Black lives did not matter. The buildings were rebuilt, but death continues to be a one-way ticket to a destination from which no one has yet returned.

As long as whites do not ask themselves about the historical, political, and cultural conditions that are the source of racial identification in the United States, the racist straitjacket will not come undone. How did a group composed of sundry European ancestry—English, Irish, Italian, French, Norwegian, German, and so on—come to form white people? How and why did the American identity and white identity become synonymous, interchangeable, normative, and exclusive? The different groups retained their ethnic identity in the private sphere but became white in the public sphere to benefit from the advantages of the dominant–dominated relationship. White identity is founded on racism.

I am not a race and neither are you. Humans are not concepts. We are defined by the relationship we establish with one another. It is not a racial relationship. The way we treat or mistreat each other reflects who we are as human beings.

The racial designation is rooted in a rhetoric of dehumanization, dispossession, property, and enjoyment. As long as relations of domination exist, it cannot be renounced. Historically speaking, we know who "owned the Blacks." The question we must now ask is: What took hold of the conscience of the people who took ownership of them? We can say, with Aimé Césaire, that oppressive practices such as slavery and colonization will dehumanize even the most civilized man, "who, in order to ease his conscience gets into the habit of seeing the other man as *an animal*, accustoms himself to treating him like an animal, and tends objectively to transform *himself* into an animal."[8]

Racism is a double-edged sword. Because white America had to get used to its violence against Black people, it hardened to their suffering. Blacks are insufficiently diagnosed and their pain is often disregarded. In 2017, a white police officer stopped a white woman on the highway. In a state of panic, the woman confessed that she had seen videos of police violence. In an attempt no doubt to reassure her, the policeman replied: "But you're not Black. Remember, we only kill Black people."[9]

Suffering is human. Sooner or later we all endure it. Given that human beings are beings of relationships, the universality of suffering cannot be proclaimed in the absence of reciprocal recognition. Unfortunately, this recognition is cruelly lacking. I understand the suffering of the other when I identify with the person.

---

8 Aimé Césaire, *Discourse on Colonialism* (Joan Pinkham trans.) (New York: Monthly Review Press, 1972), p. 41.

9 Lindsey Bever and Andrew deGrandpre, "'We Only Kill Black People,' a Cop Told a Woman—On Camera. Now He'll Lose His Job," *Washington Post*, September 1, 2017. Available at: https://wapo.st/3hI9PiA (last accessed on August 26, 2020).

Because I imagine myself in that person's shoes, compassion turns into duty. I offer assistance to the person who is suffering. I find the strength and courage to come to their aid.

The twenty-four-hour news channels have turned the suffering of Black Americans into a gruesome spectacle. Although mass killings occur regularly, white bodies are never observed the same way. Out of concern for the human being's dignity and respect, they are not subjected to dehumanizing overexposure. In watching victims whom the police treat like wild animals, white America savors the pornographic violence. The Black individual is forced to examine his existence through the lens of gratuitous death and unpunished crime. Paradoxically, although he is not responsible for the denial of his own humanity, the victim must solve the problem created by his tormentor: an impossible mission.

On a Sunday morning, September 15, 1963, members of the Ku Klux Klan murdered four girls in a Baptist church in Birmingham, Alabama. On June 17, 2015, Dylann Roof shot at close range people participating in a Bible study group, taking the lives of nine of them in Charleston, South Carolina. This racist massacre took place in a church, one of the founding members of which was Denmark Vesey, the man who bought his freedom and was later hanged for organizing a slave revolt in the same town.

In 1899, James Weldon Johnson wrote: "We have come over a way that with tears has been watered, we have come, treading our path through the blood of the slaughtered."[10] Over fifty years ago,

---

10 These words are from the poem "Lift Every Voice and Sing" written by James Weldon Johnson in 1900 and set to music by his brother John Rosamond Johnson five years later. The National Association for the Advancement of Colored People made it into the Black National Anthem.

Nina Simone sang "Mississippi Goddam," lending her voice to the fight for civil rights. In 2015, Kendrick Lamar's song "Alright" became the hymn of Black Lives Matter. Forging a language that improvises on the cracks of existence is a prerequisite for self-examination, spiritual endurance, radical transformation, and brotherly love: "Love is patient, love is kind. It does not envy, it does not boast, it is not proud. It does not dishonor others, it is not self-seeking, it is not easily angered, it keeps no record of wrongs. Love does not delight in evil but rejoices with the truth. It always protects, always trusts, always hopes, always perseveres."[11]

The power that redeems from chaos manifests itself when we persist in creating a new language that expresses the complexity of hope in the face of despair, love in the face of hate, and faith in humanity even though men and women have disappointed us many times and continue to do so.

The Haitian Revolution, anti-colonial struggles, the civil rights movement, the prophetic words and deeds of assassinated leaders are moments of eternity that changed the face of the world. Black suns burst through the heaps of junk with which they were covered.

Our collective history defines us, but aren't we also more than what it makes of us? Donald Trump wants to make America great again. Are we facing a return to the darkest hours of American history? Is the color of nostalgia white?

Four centuries ago, the first African captives arrived in Jamestown, Virginia. African American populations were reduced to slavery for 245 years. They have been free for 155 years. Do slaves and their descendants reflect the greatness of America? If freedom

---

11 1 Corinthians 13:4–8.

in this country is inseparable from the massacre of Native Americans, the confiscation of their land, and the subjugation of people of sub-Saharan origin for profit, then we are subjected to a vision of freedom that puts us in chains. It condemns non-white populations to oppression.

How can I be free when I enslave you?
How can you be free when you make me a slave?
How can I be free when I colonize you?
How can you be free when I am colonized?

I am breaking with an imperialist conception of humanity and freedom. Following the example of Walter Mignolo, I invite you to practice "epistemic disobedience" and reject the kind of Eurocentric particularism that claims to be universal. It is important to decolonize the production of knowledge about being and becoming. From the outset, the declaration of human rights excluded non-white individuals.

Matthew Ajibade
Tanisha Anderson
Sandra Bland
Yvette Smith
Aiyana Stanley-Jones
Michael Brown
Jordan Davis
Eric Garner

Akai Gurley

Charley Keunang

Trayvon Martin

Laquan McDonald

Tamir Rice

Walter Scott

Philando Castile

Botham Jean

Atatiana Jefferson

Ahmaud Arbery

Breonna Taylor

Rayshard Brooks

George Floyd

And many others remain excluded from the great story of freedom and human rights. At the intersection of injustice and violence, hope wavers.

> "The very time I thought I was lost,
> My dungeon shook and my chains fell off."[12]

A slave uttered these words. If tears last a night, a new joy[13] comes in the morning. Witnesses have crossed the Valley of Tears. They accompany posterity toward its destiny. The struggle continues ...

---

12 Baldwin, *The Fire Next Time*, p. 32.

13 Roy Hargrove, "A New Joy" in *Diamond in the Rough*, CD (New York: RCA Legacy, 1990).

"I can't breathe. I can't breathe. I can't breathe."[14]

Are you breathing? Are we breathing?

I can't breathe. I can't breathe. I can't breathe.

As a nation, as citizens, as human beings, our collective courageous choices and our cowardice give rise to the world in which we live.

Together we will survive or perish.

---

14 This is what Eric Garner said during his fatal arrest in New York City on July 17, 2014. Six years later, George Floyd uttered the same words.

The Futile Sound of Black Agony

I can't breathe. Ah! I will probably just die this way.

George Floyd [1]

One hand in his pocket, Derek Chauvin pressed his knee into George Floyd's neck for 7 minutes and 46 seconds.[2] Gasping, the unfortunate man stammered out his deceased mother's name, thought of his children, and begged for mercy from his murderer: "I'm through, I'm through. I'm claustrophobic. My stomach hurts. My neck hurts. Everything hurts. I need some water or something, please. Please? I can't breathe, officer." Chauvin wore a sardonic smirk. Deaf and blind to Floyd's distress, sneering, he retorted: "Then stop talking, stop yelling, it takes a heck of a lot of oxygen

---

1 The transcript drawn from the body cameras of the policemen implicated in the arrest of George Floyd was filed at a Minnesota district court on July 7, 2020. Available at: https://bit.ly/3jLgIR4 (last accessed on September 7, 2020). Following quotes are taken from the same transcript.

2 Minnesota prosecutors acknowledged that Chauvin had his knee on the neck of George Floyd for 7 minutes, 46 seconds, not the 8:46 that has become a symbol of police brutality.

to talk." Surrounded by his uniformed accomplices, the police officer put real effort into the work. The tormenter felt sadistic pleasure as his entire weight crushed Floyd's neck. The anger and concern of bystanders over the cruelty of his act troubled him not in the slightest.

After 7 minutes and 46 seconds, an eternity, the man on the ground exhaled his last breath. The crowd's horrified cries and expressions of empathy echoed in the dungeon of helplessness. George Floyd fell forever silent. The futile sound of his agony ended. Chauvin was done with his dirty work. An inquiry about a counterfeit 20-dollar bill concluded with a homicide in broad daylight.

On May 25, 2020 George Floyd joined the community of Black victims of police violence. This tragedy, so commonplace in America's disadvantaged neighborhoods, took on an extraordinary global resonance.

Black Lives Matter

Las vidas negran importan

La vie des Noirs compte

Mas'alat Hayat Alsuwd

From Minneapolis to Paris, by way of London, Rio de Janeiro, Accra, Tokyo, Madrid, Ramallah, and Sydney, the public execution of George Floyd set off an unprecedented, planetwide anger against racism. It became the visual proof of centuries-old oppression. Declaring that silence is violence, whites, more numerous than usual, took to the streets of American cities. Doped up on the steroids of social justice, some went from moral apathy to a moralizing hysteria.

Out of solidarity, out of opportunism in plenty of cases, the collective indignation turned into an international antiracist awakening. It echoed in Australia where Aboriginals remain the prime targets of police brutality. In the Arab Muslim world, Lebanese singer Tania Saleh, Moroccan actor Mariam Hussein, and Algerian singer Souhila Ben Lachhab posted themselves on social networks in blackface.[3] This appropriation of Black bodies in the name of the antiracist struggle lifted the veil on the persistent Arab Muslim anti-Black racism that is normally not in the spotlight. Often victim of the entire world's indifference, the oppressed Black minority of the Maghreb and the Middle East made its voice heard. Not to be outdone, sub-Saharan Africa did its part. The denunciation of George Floyd's fate led to a violent critique of the post-colonial police state.

Horrified by the phenomenon of a planetwide contagion, several European countries were rudely awakened from an amnesia matched only by the denial of justice that they had so complacently perpetrated. The populations of the former colonial empires protested against police violence and racism. In England as in the United States, historical figures with a dubious past fell from their pedestals. Written in red paint on the statue of Jean-Baptiste Colbert, the words "négrophobie d'État," meaning State negrophobia, enraged the idolaters of a France so proud of its great men that it cannot tolerate anyone mussing their image. Not for the first time, the statue of a former prime minister and English war hero found itself adorned with the words "Churchill was racist."

---

3 See Nadda Osman, "'Blackface' Arab Stars Spark Backlash over Tasteless Solidarity with US Protests," *Middle East Eye*, June 3, 2020. Available at: https://bit.ly/3i8c6nt (last accessed on September 7, 2020).

Across Belgium, monuments dedicated to King Leopold II were roughed up.

Participants in the oppressive and racist machine—the beneficiaries of unabashed capitalism—rode the wave of racial discontent. Formerly piqued by Colin Kaepernick's activism, to the point of ending his career, the National Football League (NFL) condemned the systematic oppression of and racism against Black people.[4] Uber, Netflix, Amazon, Apple, Facebook, and Google all rebranded themselves. Taking million-dollar steps in the struggle against racism, creating jobs for Black people without forgetting the ostentatious stamping of the phrase Black Lives Matter on their websites, these businesses successfully combined aggressive marketing strategies and the quest for social justice. This neoliberal co-opting of the revolt of the marginalized did not particularly shock anyone. It was even applauded. Donning its humanitarian and virtuous costume, the capitalist behemoth presented itself, yet again, as the solution to a problem in which it is an active participant.

If it is possible to take some enjoyment from the birth of a movement for social justice, we need also to recognize a certain distress in the fact that racial polarization and ideological binaries tend toward the destruction of shared human understanding. Whites take a knee and lie flat on their bellies for noble or dubious reasons. Antifascists objectify riots. Fanatics of morally upright antiracism

---

4 NFL commissioner Roger Goodell recognized the wrongs done by his organization and on its behalf expressed condolences to the families of George Floyd, Breonna Taylor, and Ahmaud Arbery. See "Roger Goodell Issues Statement on Death of George Floyd, Nationwide Protests," NFL.com, May 30, 2020. Available at: https://bit.ly/3byF8Kx (last accessed on September 7, 2020).

call for the banishment of moderates who oppose their religion. White supremacists fuss about the menace of tyrant minorities. They have all got to say their piece. A furious madness is taking hold. Arguing that the time had come to recognize the difference between race and ethnicity,[5] the *New York Times* chose to spell the word *black* with a capital B.[6] The National Museum of African American History and Culture published a controversial chart about whiteness that it withdrew after having made a public apology.[7]

Out of solidarity with Black Lives Matter, Rebecca Walkowitz, English Department chair at Rutgers University, decided to decolonialize the curriculum. The inclusion of African American literature in the list of courses required for an English major went along with the inclusion of new obligatory material centered on literature of the Global South. While these measures are praise-worthy and necessary, the idea of incorporating "critical grammar" in their pedagogy is disturbing. The goal is to question the dogma of teaching writing by emphasizing grammar and sentence struc-ture. According to Walkowitz, her department's initiative will avoid causing disadvantage to populations from multilingual backgrounds

---

5 It is worth noting that such capitalization already applied to groups such as Latinx, Asian, and Native American.

6 Nancy Coleman, "Why We're Capitalizing Black", Times Insider, *New York Times*, July 5, 2020. Available at: https://nyti.ms/3jWNDCn (last accessed on September 7, 2020).

7 This chart affirmed notably that individualism, the nuclear family, work ethic, punctuality, delayed gratification, politeness, and respect for authority were values particular to whites. These affirmations are excerpted from a book written by Judith H. Katz, one of the pioneers of antiracist literature written by whites and for whites: *White Awareness: Handbook for Anti-Racism Training* (Norman: University of Oklahoma Press, 1978).

or with little exposure to normalized, "academic" English. It will also contribute to the eradication of systemic inequalities that Blacks, Native Americans, and people of color must confront.[8] Attacking traditional grammar in order to resolve the problem of racism? When you give someone a hammer, everything starts to look like a nail.

As a Black French-speaking woman who has lived in the United States for twenty years and who speaks, writes, and teaches in English, when I use this language, I have the impression of driving a Formula 1 race car and risking an accident at any second. I still cannot get it to adapt to my needs. Every day, I try to improve.

Early on, I would not say what I wanted to say but what I could say. During this period of my existence, I became mute. I would hear: "That's not American English." My interlocutors would often correct me. Brilliant when I would express myself in French, I had the impression that some form of grotesque stupidity took hold of my brain as soon as I had to speak in English. It was a total regression and one that undoubtedly affected my ego. Sometimes, when a word's meaning escapes you, the discomfort that you try to disguise makes you smile. I understood this truth when I was twenty-four. Content without form led to incomprehension, to misunderstandings, to frustration, to verbal escalation, to violence.

The Black American writers I admire infuse the language of Shakespeare with their own cultural heritage.[9] Knowing a language

8 Rutgers English Department News, "Department Actions in Solidarity with Black Lives Matter," Rutgers School of Arts and Sciences, June 19, 2020. Available at: https://bit.ly/3jQ8xCY (last accessed on September 7, 2020).

9 It should be emphasized that the action taken by Rutgers University is not a continuation of the debates on the recognition and valorization of Black American

allows you to understand the world you live in. It also provides tools that are necessary to establish relationships with others. Instead of getting rid of grammar, we should reform how it is learned from elementary school on, to get away from any rigid or austere approach, and to include cultural components at the level of content, to develop the idea of grammar in real situations. For many years, I taught French to American students. Their weaknesses in understanding English grammar complicated their learning of a foreign language. One of my colleagues, a professor of Spanish, said that she had observed the same thing.

Not race but social conditions are responsible for the linguistic disparities between citizens of the same country. An education that promotes levelling from the bottom in the name of egalitarianism will have disastrous consequences for marginalized populations. It leads to a racist antiracism: a way of essentializing and accommodating deficiencies wrongly attributed to groups whose ultimate desire is to learn.

The current antiracist ideology is anchored in an insurmountable paradox: the desire to fix racism reinforces the assignment of identities. Good whites punish the bad. In the wake of the revolt that shook America after George Floyd's death, *White Fragility: Why It's So Hard to Talk about Black People*[10] by Robin DiAngelo

---

English as a separate language. There is abundant critical literature on that subject. See, for example, J. L. Dillard, *Black English: Its History and Usage in the United States* (New York: Random Hourse, 1972), Geneva Smitherman, *Black Talk: Words and Phrases from the Hood to the Amen Corner* (New York: Houghton Mifflin, 2000), John Russel Rickford and Russel John Rickford, *Spoken Soul: The Story of Black English* (New York: John Wiley and Sons, 2000).

10 Robin DiAngelo, *White Fragility: Why It's So Hard to Talk about Black People* (with a foreword by Michael Eric Dyson) (Boston, MA: Beacon Press, 2018).

had an unprecedented success. This book provides antiracism with its new credo. The media are all talking about it and white people buy it or recommend it without having read a word. The author has been everywhere on television. Without any notion of the destiny that awaited it, I had included this book on the reading list for a course entitled "Introduction to Race and Ethnicity" that I taught in the summer of 2020. To see *White Fragility* elevated to the rank of an antiracist Bible or else lambasted for its anti-white[11] or anti-Black racism[12] left me perplexed.

A former university professor, Robin DiAngelo is now famous for her work in the diversity industry. Before becoming a sought-after public speaker known for her costly services, she directed business workshops on implicit biases and racism. DiAngelo affirms beyond the shadow of a doubt that all white people are racist. Consequently, they must dedicate their existence to expiating a sin that is consubstantial with their identity. DiAngelo is an apologist for contrition. The argumentation gets lost in the messianic exaltation of the self-mortified white body. The author describes, nevertheless, certain coping mechanisms of self-defense and conscious or unconscious protection that make whites uneasy about the question of racism.

The bitter criticism levelled against DiAngelo reveals the shortcomings of an approach that focuses on behavioral problems

---

11 Matt Taibbi, "On 'White Fragility': A Few Thoughts on America's Smash-Hit #1 Guide to Egghead Racism," Reporting by Matt Taibbi, June 29, 2020. Available on: https://bit.ly/2R0KSmT (last accessed on September 7, 2020).

12 John McWhorter, "The Dehumanizing Condescension of *White Fragility*: The Popular Book Aims to Combat Racism but Talks Down to Black People," *Atlantic*, July 15, 2020. Available at: https://bit.ly/3bBiGQU (last accessed on September 7, 2020).

and on creating a welcoming workplace. The antiracist awakening is above all else didactic and prescriptive. It resembles a mandatory emotional-torture session. The historical context serves as a mere backdrop. The participants must confess their racism while suffering *ad hominem* attacks. The irony of this situation is that absolution is impossible. Is the goal to combat racism or to train individuals so that the business can blithely function with a clean conscience?

Whether they are Republican, Democrat, or from the moderate left, the majority of DiAngelo's detractors get shrill because she calls them irredeemable racists. In her antiracist breviary, even when whites fight the good fight, all is lost from the start. As a result, whites must constantly strain to become the best possible allies. DiAngelo and her disciples do not recognize the inherent asymmetry in relations of solidarity with the oppressed. Contrary to appearances, these relations do not create equality. They produce an inverse power dynamic. To be a good ally means submitting to the dictates of the oppressed person. Subjugated by external injunctions, this identity is fundamentally defective. By definition, the ally is always susceptible to correction, discipline, or loss of ally status. These alienating labels should be rejected and make way for a vocabulary establishing the humanity of all.

Following the George Floyd Affair, the debate on free speech and against "cancel culture" has returned with a vengeance. Formerly confined to the ideological furor of students and certain leftist professors on American campuses, these practices—denunciation, humiliation, boycott, and power to silence certain figures of the political world, the intelligentsia, or the entertainment industry—are now making their mark outside of universities. The hunt for personae non gratae has been causing havoc in newsrooms. Having refused to submit to the doxa of the moment, certain journalists of the *New York Times* resigned. Fearful of getting burned at the stake of group think, some professors and students avoid expressing dissident opinions publicly. Confronted by the crowd of the woke, it is better to keep a low profile.[13] Conscious of the ravages of the woke imperative, more than 150 intellectuals signed "A Letter on Justice and Open Debate" addressing the dangers of censorship and of ideological intimidation from the zealots of social and racial justice.[14] In arguing for de-escalation, they provoked an uproar. A group of journalists and academics vigorously denounced the editorial that appeared in *Harper's Magazine*. They reproached the publication for having privileged the opinion of established writers of whom the majority were white, male, and cisgender. Their letter

---

13 According to Samuel Veissière and Anne-Sophie Chazaud: "The term 'woke' is first used unironically by militants of the New Left who claim to be 'awake' to the power mechanisms of the cultural institutions that they perceive as 'colonial,' especially as far as genders and the statuses of ethnic and sexual minorities are concerned. [...] The culture of social-justice warriors traces its origin to American departments of social sciences where postmodernism has dominated for almost twenty years. The first 'French' connection with this phenomenon is as ironic as it is perverse. Postmodernism, at the origin of the Woke movement and especially associated with the works of Foucault, Deleuze, and Derrida, is termed 'French theory' in America. In its current ambitions, this philosophical current that questions the hegemonic dimensions of received ideas is strongly marked by an Anglo-Saxon Calvinist puritanism that seeks to safeguard 'purity' and sees victims and villains everywhere" ("Etes-vous contaminé par l'épidémie de 'woke' [ça n'est pas parce que vous ne savez pas ce que c'est que vous n'êtes pas concerné]?" *Atlantico*, October 6, 2020. Available at: https://bit.ly/3lZHIyf; last accessed on September 7, 2020.)

14 *Harper's Magazine*, "A Letter on Justice and Open Debate," July 7, 2020. Available at: https://bit.ly/2DzTcXF (last accessed on September 7, 2020).

referred neither to the question of power nor to the editorial practices that reduce marginalized populations to silence.[15]

Within the community of Black American activists, the war of the sexes was declared: "#SayHerName." Different factions laid into each other on Twitter and Facebook. Black feminists were troubled by the lack of interest given to female victims of police violence.[16] Why should Breonna Taylor not receive as much attention as George Floyd? It is a question of statistics, the opposing side replied. The police killed more Black men than women. The slogans "All Black Lives Matter" and "BlackTransLivesMatter" appeared on social networks in order to include members of the LGBTQI community. The prevailing discourse did not take into account the double victimization of transgender individuals at the hands of Black men and of policemen. A macabre competition was held among populations marginalized because of their race, class, gender, and sexual orientation. A hierarchy of victimization encouraged violent and obscene debates. Which group would captivate the white gaze? Who would take home the trophy of supreme victim?

---

15 *The Objective*, "A More Specific Letter on Justice and Open Debate," July 10, 2020. Available at: https://bit.ly/2GDkWvN (last accessed on September 7, 2020).

16 Brittney Cooper, "Why Are Black Women and Girls Still an Afterthought in Our Outrage over Police Violence," *Time*, June 4, 2020; available at: https://bit.ly/3jXGGkt (last accessed on September 7, 2020). Kimberlé Crenshaw, "The Urgency of Intersectionality," *TEDWomen 2016*, October 2016; available at: https://bit.ly/3bxhezf (last accessed on September 7, 2020). Kimberley Foster, "Why I Will Not March for Eric Garner", *For Harriet*, July 22, 2014; available at: https://bit.ly/3bxaiCh (last accessed on September 7, 2020).

Invisibility of some; hypervisibility of others. The truth none-theless is elsewhere. Until proven otherwise, the media's over-exposure of violence inflicted on Black men does not improve the existence of those who remain alive. It reveals the precariousness of an existence constantly subject to the power of death.[17] TV screens, t-shirts, murals, and social networks immortalize victims. Only death accords to these individuals the right to be remembered in the social imaginary. Before their lives ended on the asphalt, who were they? Was anyone interested in their dreams, in their states of mind? Haloed with postmortem fame as heroes and martyrs, the deceased symbolize the oppression of people of African descent in imperialist democracies.

Rather than get entangled in competitive victimhood, better reflect coldly on the problem posed by a necrophile system of recognition grounded in an insatiable "appetite for the death of black men."[18] Neoliberal activism keeps up an incestuous relation-ship with necropolitics.[19] What is the significance of the state's ritualized violence against Blacks in the social, economic, and cultural ecosystem of America? It is always Black bodies that the media toss out as fodder to public opinion. The suffering of Blacks in the United States is a singular spectacle and it has been going

17 J.-A. Mbembé, "Necropolitics" (Libby Meintjes trans.), *Public Culture* 15(1) (Winter 2003): 11–40; here, p. 12.

18 Tommy J. Curry, "Why Does America Have an Appetite for the Death of Black Men?" *PBS News Hour*, August 10, 2017. Available at: https://to.pbs.org/-3i6qWuJ (last accessed on September 7, 2020).

19 Mbembé asks: "But under what practical conditions is the right to kill, to allow to live, or to expose to death exercised? Who is the subject of this right?" ("Necropolitics," p. 12)

on for more than 400 years. The nation watches a tragedy of its own authorship. Where slaves had a market value in a plantation economy, their descendants inherit a devalued citizenship.

At the end of the spring of 2020, George Floyd's death interrupted the morbid litany that recited on a daily basis the number of deaths due to Covid-19. While at the start of the pandemic the tragedy's color was white, after a few weeks it became Black. Stupefied, America announced the death rate of a population whose precariousness nonetheless explained its extreme vulnerability to the virus. Floyd's autopsy revealed that, in addition to being positive for a number of illegal substances, he had contracted Covid-19. The public execution of this man and the sickness's devastating effect on the heart of the Black American community revealed nothing that we did not already know. [20]

In light of the racial, social, and health climate, what society will emerge from the current upheavals? What must we do now?

Let us not repeat the pattern of totalitarian thought of which we have been the victims. The creation of an equitable world will never happen at the cost of liberty and respect for the humanity of all. We must distinguish between justice and vengeance, between struggle for equality and will to power. Understand and accept that the Earth is our inheritance. We must share and protect it. It is incumbent upon us to create a language capable of communicating

---

20 In Chicago, for example, Black Americans represent 30 percent of the city's inhabitants but 68 percent of the death rate. They are dying from the Coronavirus six times more than whites. See Cecilia Reyes, Nausheen Husain, Christy Gutowski, Stacy St. Clair, and Gregory Pratt, "Chicago's Coronavirus Disparity: Black Chicagoans Are Dying at Nearly Six Times the Rate White Residents, Data Show," *Chicago Tribune*, April 7, 2020. Available at: https://bit.ly/358a0R4 (last accessed on September 7, 2020).

human experience without reproducing, in the name of inclusion, mechanisms of alienation and exclusion.

Capitalism incessantly worsens racial and social inequalities. Standing on a mountain of dead bodies, democratic imperialist law and order are wavering. Unhappiness for some can no longer mean happiness for others.

What does the future hold? The best, or the worst.